'As ever, Tim is thorough in his theology, honest in his reflections and practical in his application. I trust that this book will be a great encouragement to many.'

Gareth Lloyd-Jones

Team Leader, Kinetic Network and Senior Pastor, Ridgeway Community Church, South Oxfordshire

'I know my friend Tim Tucker's previous book *Grief and Grace* has been a help and encouragement to many. Similarly, I'm sure this precious book birthed from going through the fire of deep grief and pain and yet being able to come out the other side refined, stronger and more able to help others, will be greatly used. One thing's for sure, all of us sooner or later will need to hear the words of wisdom and encouragement held within. I'm sure you will be encouraged and heartened, as I was, as you dig in to these powerful life lessons and scriptural principles.'

Andy Hawthorne OBE

Founder and Global CEO, The Message Trust

'Martin Heidegger, a well-known, unbelieving philosopher, wrote that knowledge about death helps us to understand the reason for our existence. Jesus came to bring us that knowledge. Yet as Tim writes, Christians avoid talking about death. Following his first book *Grief and Grace*, written after the tragic death of his young wife, *Finding Life After Death* reflects upon what he has learned himself and from many who have contacted him since the publication of that book. It deals with a difficult subject but uses up-to-date terminology and is easy to read. If you are searching for answers about life and death, this is the book to read.'

Dr Roger Tucker

Emeritus Presbyterian Minister, University Research Fellow (UFS) and South African Theological Seminary Associate

'Who better to write this book than someone who has faced the reality of grief? Tim addresses things in this book you don't think about if you've not experienced them. Life is terminal, death will come to us all and not to talk about it and the effects it has on the people we leave, seems ridiculous particularly when it's unexpected. What we know is that we have the hope of heaven and a future to come if we know Jesus. That for me is the thing I hold on to and something that Tim expresses so clearly in this book.'

Danielle Campsall

Chief Administration Officer, The Message Trust

'If you are grieving, then Tim wants to help you. Having experienced profound grief recently, he has empathy for you, and he knows that grief, especially grief around the death of a loved one, can wear you down and wear you out. To get through it you need more than an understanding nod or an encouraging word. You need more than practical tips and emotional exercises. You need the hope, love and power that only God can provide. But when you're grieving, God may seem far away. In this short but powerful book you'll find the hope that will help you through.'

Chris Bolinger

Author, *Daily Strength for Men* & *52 Weeks of Strength for Men*

'In 2021 I lost both my older siblings, my sister and my brother in just six months. Tim's book Grief and Grace, was literally heaven sent for me. It helped me more than I can describe. In his new book, *Finding Life After Death* Tim takes this a few steps further. He encourages us powerfully and practically, to maintain a biblical perspective, (or maybe adopt one), to see death in a new light. I highly recommend it, and hope it will be a great encouragement to you too. After all, we all will have to face the realisation that death is part of the cycle of life.'

Paul Hallam

Founder and Senior Pastor of The Lighthouse Church Network, Manchester UK, and Director of Lighthouse International Ministries

'*Finding Life After Death* is a small wisdom book, a statement of paradox and a mystical unity between sorrow and joy, loss and gain, grief and glory. The book gently and forcefully reminds us of Solomon's wise words "it is better to go to a house of mourning than to go to a house of feasting, for death is the destiny of everyone, the living should take this to heart" (Ecclesiastes 7:2) It's in a house of mourning that one has moments to think seriously about the meaning and brevity of life. Tim, from personal experience boldly speaks about living to die and dying to live, only possible through faith in Jesus Christ who died so that all who believe in him may live forever.'

Dr. Bekele Shanko

Vice President, Campus Crusade for Christ International and author of *Never Alone: From Ethiopian Villager to Global Leader*

'Death is a difficult topic to speak about. But Tim does so with theological richness and with a pastoral posture. This is an important book because we will all deal with death or in the mean time, know many people who are grieving. This book will give handles on how to navigate the rough waters of grief and death.'

Luxolo Kentane
National Director, Alpha South Africa, and Founder of Living Legacy Movement

'What a powerful story of God's everlasting and redeeming love weaved into the reality of deep loss. Tim's narrative captures his personal journey through the endured pain of grief and loss, one that does not travel in a linear manner but moves forwards and backwards as Jesus captures our hearts and faithfully offers us abundant life through his promises and his love. As I reflected deeply (as Tim advises us) on "life after death" eventually the penny dropped – true life and living is only found in Jesus Christ. I would recommend this book to all of us without a doubt!'

Dr Dianne Matthews
MBChB (Wits), HDip (Fam Med), HDip (Obstetrics), PgDip (Health Sciences Education)

'Like many family doctors over the years I realise the truth in what Tim shares here. Death is our least-prepared-for major life experience, coming unannounced and threatening to over-whelm us. We struggle with our own sorrows, as well as those whose pain is raw and whose questions appear unanswerable. I am grateful for these ideas and reflections. Tim has gathered real stories, thoughtful deliberations and biblical perspectives from his own journey through grief, witnessing to the possibility of renewal and hope. I commend Tim's work to all who are looking to find a faithful guide to *Finding Life After Death*.

Dr John Patterson MA(Cantab.) MRCP MRCGP
Associate Medical Director NHS Greater Manchester

FINDING

LIFE

AFTER

DEATH

a (biblical) survivor's guide

TIM TUCKER

the message

First published in Great Britain in 2023 by The Message Trust.
The Message Trust
Lancaster House, Harper Road
Manchester, M22 4RG, UK

ISBN 978-1-7393073-4-9
eISBN 978-1-7393073-5-6

Cover design and typesetting: Simon Baker, Thirteen Creative

To Christina

Finding life with you has brought me unexpected and unimaginable love and joy.

We will not be shaken. Psalm 62:1–2

CONTENTS

FOREWORD

MAHLATSE MASHUA

When Tim asked me to write a foreword for this book, my heart sank because I knew that I could not do it faithfully without confronting myself.

I have known him as a friend and a mentor and have tracked his journey with grief very closely. Recently, when a friend suddenly lost his wife to cancer, leaving him with three young children, I was grateful for Tim's generosity and courage in sharing his story and processing his emotions in his first book, *Grief and Grace*, as we could use it as a guide to navigate the perilous waters of grief. This is one of the stories you will encounter in this book.

It is one thing to stand with someone in their grief as a consoling partner when tragedy strikes. It is another thing entirely to face your own grief.

About three years ago, a man I considered a mentor passed away following a short illness. His death revealed the pedestal I had placed him on, fuelled by my admiration and gratitude.

I had learned so much from him and had looked forward to learning more. His death was a dagger to my heart because I had taken his continued presence in my life as a certainty, not really having contemplated something different. Like me, many mourned his passing and shared how they had been deeply impacted by his life. Shortly after his death, an investigator's report revealed and concluded that my mentor had been guilty of abusing women and of living a life that contradicted the message that he taught and was well-known for. The painful testimonies of women dealt a blow to the image I had of this man and I was faced with the second death, that of my mentor as I had known him.

I then watched as the organisation I loved, composed of diverse communities worldwide, crumbled. I observed colleagues striving to reimagine their future, some, sadly, at the expense of integrity and godly character. I watched friendships that were seemingly forged by 'heaven' fall apart, and friends who were inseparable, frame each other in ways that made reconciliation a pipe dream. I watched as many were forced to relive their own woundedness from their pasts as the themes in the revelations resembled their personal stories of abuse. I watched as we, known for being courageous in giving thoughtful answers to life's tough questions, lost our collective voice and credibility to give a response to many who found new questions in the story.

During this time, I became involved in starting and leading a charity organisation that had, and continues to have, a profound impact on under-resourced communities. I got involved in leading peace-making and mediation efforts within corporations, schools, and sporting teams. I picked up qualifications in negotiations and dispute resolution, sports management and earned my Master's degree in International Affairs (Cybersecurity).

One day, my wife held my hand and with all the love and gentleness in her eyes, looked at me and said, 'You have and are doing well with all your academic and professional accomplishments. But I think it's also time that you hear that you are running away from your own grief. You are running at a fast pace doing really good things, but I think you are afraid of slowing down lest your broken heart catches up to you.' On that very day, I received a text from Tim, asking me to write a foreword to his book. My heart sank.

From Tim's previous book, I learnt that without a proper guide, grief can become the uninvited guest who refuses to be ignored, outpaced, or willed away. She doesn't heed the hints from one's overly subscribed calendar nor does she regard the library of intellectual answers one can muster in a philosophy class. Instead, she colludes with time to lodge herself deep in the crevices of one's soul, casting long, lingering shadows on the familiar – on the laughter that once danced effortlessly in the room, on the simple joy of morning coffee, on the comforting hug of a routine day. She imposes herself on the contours of the known, turning bright days grey, and in her wake, leaves a quiet dissonance that reverberates through the mundane, constantly reminding one of her unyielding presence. You can't outrun grief.

As I read the manuscript, I received a fresh invitation to walk with God through a chapter in my life that I had wished many times would just be erased in time. I received fresh courage to ask my questions anew, questions that I had buried underneath layers of intellectual soil. I paused when Tim gently asked the reader to reflect on the major thoughts in every chapter. I prayed honest prayers and admitted that I needed God to help me mourn appropriately.

Tim writes, 'Death is painful for those that remain. No matter how we try to explain it, rationalise it or theologise about it, death is painful. And the counsel the Bible provides is that mourning is a righteous and necessary response to death.'

As you read on, may you hear the voice that validates your anguish, connects you to meaning during a painful season and gives you a vision of God's 'life after death'.

Mahlatse Mashua
Autumn 2023

INTRODUCTION

In 2019 I released my personal story of loss in the book, *Grief and Grace* which is an account of my journey through grief after the sudden loss of my wife in 2016. As I have engaged with many people about grief and loss since 2019, I felt called to write a follow-up book for the following three interrelated reasons.

Firstly, the response to *Grief and Grace* was overwhelmingly positive. Sharing my story has enabled others to articulate their own feelings as they continue to journey through grief. Many people identified with the language I used to express the void and confusion that grief can plunge people into. Men particularly seemed to find it helpful. I have spoken to numerous men who have struggled to express the pain of their grief. My story seemed to give men a license to share their own story which is a huge step towards healing. I also found that *Grief and Grace* helped people to deal with many kinds of grief, not just grief relating to the death of a loved one.

The second reason emanates from this. As I've engaged with people and heard so many stories of pain and loss, I have been inspired by the faith that so many believers demonstrate during unbelievably painful experiences. The Christian message of life after death is not 'pie in the sky'… but makes a tangible difference to how we experience life after the death of a loved one. Hence the play on words in the title of this book. Grief changes us and remains part of us in some shape or form. However, God can work in the process of our grief to bring us into a better understanding of himself and a deeper appreciation of his love and grace. God can redeem our pain. And yet, so little is written or taught on how to discover this perspective when we are going through grief and loss. When we filmed the Grief and Grace video series, so many gems of learning came from the people we interviewed that I believed more could still be written about finding life after death.

Thirdly, the Bible has a lot to say about death. I feel that Christians are not talking about death enough. That sounds morbid, doesn't it? However, we can't escape being impacted by death and we can't escape the fact that we ourselves are mortal. We seem to struggle to navigate the paradox that both pain and hope are real and run parallel to each other. Some people focus on the pain and seem to lose hope. Others focus on the hope and bypass the necessary processes of grief. This book will go further than my own story as it seeks to develop a biblical approach to grief and loss that holds this tension together. Nevertheless, this book is meant to be accessible to anyone going through grief. Therefore, it will not be an exhaustive Bible study, but provide signposts of biblical truth that can help Christians navigate the pain in their own lives and move towards healing.

I write with the unequivocal belief in a sovereign God who can redeem our pain for his perfect purposes in our lives. That has been my experience. However, God also meets with us uniquely. This book is not a general recipe but continues with the theme that I began in *Grief and Grace*, which is to provide signposts of hope. Ultimately, these signposts are not just for us as individual Christians but also serve as our testimony to a watching world. Our faith is perhaps most at risk when we go through pain. Yet if we continue to trust faithfully in God (even if by the skin of our teeth), our faith will ultimately be vindicated and God will be glorified. This is the victory that Paul speaks about in 1 Corinthians 15:57: 'But thanks be to God! He gives us the victory through our Lord Jesus Christ.' My hope is that this book will help many people find the victory of life after death.

The book has been divided into three parts which each contain three chapters. Part One is entitled *Perspective*. This section will provide a biblical perspective on death and grief. Part Two is entitled *Pain*. This section will validate grief and pain from a biblical viewpoint, helping readers navigate the loss they are experiencing. Part Three is entitled *Purpose*. From the foundation of a biblical perspective and the practical realities of pain, this section moves the reader towards understanding what God's purposes might be as he graciously works in and through our grief. This section provides a pathway to healing and finding life after death.

PART ONE
PERSPECTIVE

CHAPTER ONE

LET'S TALK ABOUT DEATH

*'It is the unknown we fear when we look upon
death and darkness, nothing more.'*
ALBUS DUMBLEDORE[1]

BETTY'S BAY

My closest encounters with death have taken place in some beautiful locations. In 2016 I lost my first wife, Laura, to a brain aneurysm while we were on holiday at Victoria Bay.

Vic Bay is situated on the world-renowned Garden Route, about four hours from Cape Town. Her death was an unexpected and uninvited invasion of my life for which I was ill-prepared. I have written about my journey through deep grief in my book *Grief and Grace*.

Fast forward five years.

I am remarried (more on this in a later chapter), and we're on another family holiday with my brother-in-law Gareth

(Laura's brother), his wife Michelle, and their children. Betty's Bay is just ninety minutes from Cape Town. Sitting at the end of a spectacularly scenic coastal drive, as False Bay laps the rocky shores, it is an idyllic sprawling holiday village. Betty's Bay is a dream location for the more reclusive holiday makers, while also home to troops of marauding baboons and a colony of African penguins.

It's 2021 and we've just entered another Covid lockdown. The beaches have once again been closed and so we are spending more time in the holiday home than anticipated. This allowed time to reflect, not only on the past five years, but on another grief moment the family was facing.

Michelle had been fighting cancer for fourteen months. A late diagnosis meant the doctors were always on the back foot. Treatment was intense. Michelle bravely and tenaciously faced the exhausting rounds of chemotherapy. In spite of the suffering she was experiencing, they had resolutely driven from Pretoria to Cape Town to spend the Christmas holiday with us. Covid restrictions meant we hadn't seen Michelle since her diagnosis and so she was determined that we should have Christmas together. Michelle was particularly excited to meet our four-month-old baby daughter and also insisted that we decorate the holiday house, Christmas tree and all.

It was heart-breaking to see the impact that the illness and rounds of chemo had on Michelle. We longed for her healing. She believed she would be healed and often talked about her desire for their family to move to Cape Town. We would have loved to have them close by. The bonds between our families are beyond blood and borne of a history of remarkable times of joy, laced with deep losses. Yet, while trying to be full of faith, we had hushed conversations with Gareth about the *reality* of the situation. Outside of a miracle, cancer would rob Michelle of breath in this life and usher her into God's presence. We had assurance of her ultimate healing in the next life but were once again facing a future in this life that we would never have chosen.

The holiday house we were staying in had an extensive balcony that overlooked the sea. One morning, I spent some time alone on the balcony. It was not an intentional time of reflection. In fact, just the opposite. I'd noticed on Apple TV+ that there was a documentary by Bruce Springsteen on his new album. I've always been a fan of 'The Boss', and thought I'd have some 'me time' watching the programme and enjoying his music. The show was called 'Bruce Springsteen's Letter to You' and is billed as a tribute to his band, The E Street Band, following their progress as they recorded their new album.

What I hadn't realised is that his new album is primarily about death. Springsteen has been a successful rock artist since the early '70s. Much of his latest album is a reflection about people he has loved and lost throughout his life. In the programme, he poignantly explains the background to many of the songs, juxtaposed with footage of him in studio with his ageing band. With song titles like 'One Minute You're Here (Next Minute You're Gone)', 'Letter To You', 'Last Man Standing', 'The Power of Prayer', 'Ghosts' and 'I'll See You In My Dreams', you can see that he is handling some heavy topics.

Once again I was reminded that grief is a journey you continue to walk through, rather than something you simply get over. Time doesn't automatically heal. I was also struck by how transparent Springsteen was, utilising his gift and art to help him process his loss. I was impressed that he had the boldness to address topics surrounding death that many consider unmentionable.

As I listened to Springsteen I was reminded of how much death is part of life. We were once again facing this reality as a family. Someone wrote, 'to be alive is to know that death is always lurking around the corner.'[2]

THE TABOO TOPIC

Yet so few people seem to talk about it. Death is a taboo topic. And this seems to be equally true for Christians as well as unbelievers, particularly believers who have been influenced by a western worldview.

Other than at funerals, how many sermons do we hear on death? Just consider it. How many Bible studies, conferences, retreats, or concerts have you attended that have had death as their central theme? Yes, there are resources for those going through grief but should we really be waiting for disaster to happen before addressing the subject? Surely, as Christians, we need to be more proactive. Death is part of life which means it's part of our discipleship. Therefore, we need to talk about death!

As we will see in this book, the Bible is not reticent to speak about death. As God's word, we can therefore conclude that God has no issue with addressing the subject of death. In fact, one might argue that the Bible is given to us as God's response to the challenge of death.

Death entered the world because of sin. God created Adam and Eve for perfect and abundant life to be enjoyed eternally with the creator. However, life is only truly meaningful when there is choice. Robotic adherence to authority is not life. So, God gave his children choice. They could obey and trust him, or they could go against his instruction. The consequence of disobedience would be the opposite of life, namely, death (see Genesis 2:15–17). When Adam and Eve ate from the tree of the knowledge of good and evil, they were exposed not only to a whole new reality (sin and evil), but also the consequences of their choice, death, and separation from God (see Genesis 3).

By God's grace, physical death did not come immediately. In all righteousness he could have immediately cast Adam and Eve into hell. Thank God, he didn't! He mercifully allowed opportunity for forgiveness and redemption. This is the story of the rest of scripture. But the curses God placed upon Adam and Eve (and the human species they represented), demonstrated the atrophy that set in, ultimately leading to the grave. Death became a reality to be faced by every human being.

The concluding words of the curse upon Adam have been adapted to become the closing words of many funeral services, 'for dust you are and to dust you will return' (Genesis 3:19). But these were not God's final words on the subject. The narrative of

Scripture journeys through an epic story of how God triumphs over death through Jesus Christ, until (spoiler alert), 'then Death and Hell were hurled into Lake Fire' (Revelation 20:14, MSG). In other words, the consequences of the disaster that occurred in Eden has been reversed. Death has been defeated once and for all! Because of the resurrection of Jesus Christ, there is hope for us beyond the grave.

GRIEFS OF MANY KINDS

However, with the final victory in view, the Bible is realistic about the struggles we will continue to face. In the opening few sentences of his first letter, the Apostle Peter clearly articulates this seeming paradox. In 1 Peter 1:3, Peter glories in the living hope we have through Christ's resurrection. In verses 4 and 5 he goes on to underline the promise of this new life, that it is an inheritance that can never spoil or fade and one that is protected by God himself. Nothing and no one can take it from us. Verse 6 starts with rejoicing, before giving us a reality check:

'Though now for a little while you may have had to suffer grief in all kinds of trials.'

Oh Peter! Please can we skip that part. Wouldn't it be nice if we could jump straight from salvation into glory?

The implication is clear. It's not just the grief of death that we have to face but *grief in all kinds of trials*. This world will bring us grief. Whether unemployment, financial crisis, marital infidelity, the moral failure of Christian leaders, our children rejecting the faith, or suffering due to natural disasters, we will face grief in all kinds of trials. We will face grief caused by our own sinfulness and grief caused by the sins of others.

None of us is exempt.

One of my favourite authors, Frank Viola, writes:

'The Lord made clear that following Him wouldn't lead to a bed of roses. Suffering and loss are involved. He promised thorns. Unfortunately, some people today present a gospel that leaves the hard parts out. The result: Christians get offended when they realise what they've gotten into.'[3]

The question then is not *if* we are going to face grief but *how should we respond* when we go through grief in all kinds of trials?

Focusing mostly on the context of life in the shadow of physical death, this book will seek to provide a biblical perspective to help us navigate grief and loss. However, the biblical truth we are examining can also help you face other losses and build a robust theology that will enable you to retain your faith against the worst onslaught this world and the devil can throw at you.

WHAT DEFINES YOU?

Returning to the balcony in Betty's Bay, what I saw with Springsteen is that his encounters with death and grief were the *most real* experiences of his life. In the moments of grief and loss, our senses are heightened. This was my experience in the 24-hour period as my late wife departed this life. Every moment has been encased in my mind. Other experiences come and go. Even times of incredible joy and laughter do not seem to have the same neural impact as what we encounter when we lose a loved one. I would go so far as to say that our response to death can define how we live. I'm not saying this as a professional psychologist but as someone who has experienced and processed (sometimes well, sometimes not so well) grief and loss of many kinds. But more than that, since I began writing and speaking about death and grief, I've seen that so many people are stuck. Or they have created a narrative to help them cope which is divorced from the truth of scripture. Others press the grief down into the recesses of their hearts and simply don't have a mechanism to help them deal with it, let alone find grace and healing.

U2 frontman, Bono, lost his mum when he was a teenager. He writes frankly about the impact this, and other griefs, had upon him in his autobiography, *Surrender*. He draws this conclusion, 'something in me understands that until we deal with the most traumatic traumas, there's a part of us that stays at the age at which we encountered them.'[4]

I'm writing this book to help you find a pathway to become unstuck. Although drawing from my own experiences, I am ultimately going to be pointing you to the Bible as the primary medium through which we can mature as believers even through times of incredible suffering. My desire is for you to be able to face the traumatic reality of the grief you are experiencing and discover that God's love and power *can* sustain you.

It seems to me that Christians give mixed messages when talking about death. We either super-spiritualise it and focus on the eternal hope we have at the expense of recognising the trauma that death does bring. Ultimately this can be an avoidance mechanism that prevents us from dealing with the grief of losing a loved one. Or we slump into despair, even to the extent of questioning our faith and the goodness of God.

THE CORDS OF DEATH

As we saw with what the Apostle Peter wrote above, the biblical perspective is not an either/or, but far more nuanced, holding these two extremes – super-spiritualisation and despair – in tension. The biblical perspective lies somewhere in the murkier space of balancing the hope we have that Jesus has conquered death, with the reality that death is a brutal invasion into our lives, one that God never intended for us. Sometimes, when experiencing grief, we can oscillate between both extremes in the same day, or even the same hour.

The Psalms provide a reality check of how tough life can be and how we grapple with our faith in the good times and the bad. Psalm 116:3 is one example of how the psalmists did not deny the reality and difficulty that death confronts us with.

'The cords of death entangled me, the anguish of the grave came over me.'

Consider for a moment how graphic these words are. The *cords* of death *entangle* us. Death is physical and can be painful. But there is also a mental and emotional reality to be faced. The shadow of the grave can cause tremendous *anguish*.

The psalmist views death as a hunter closing in on their prey. The hunter's snare entangles their quarry, causing anxiety and anguish that all is lost. There is no possibility of escape. This provokes tremendous mental torment on top of the physical pain. As we'll see in chapter 4, the Bible does not diminish the pain of death or the agony it can cause us. Even though we're Christians and have the hope of eternal life, we do not embrace death as something of no significance for us. Becoming a Christian does not make us immune from the consequences of sin in this life. Neither are we expected to embrace pain and death as some kind of pseudo-spiritual superhero. CS Lewis wrote:

'It is hard to have patience with people who say, "There is no death" or "Death doesn't matter". There is death. And whatever is matters. And whatever happens has consequences, and it and they are irrevocable and irreversible.'[5]

TO DIE IS GAIN

And yet, that is not the end of the story. The Apostle Paul, when facing his own potential execution, wrote, 'For me to live is Christ and to die is gain.' (Philippians 1:21). These are incredible words of faith and I trust that when I approach my own demise one day, I will be able to see that *death is gain*. But even Paul concluded that his job on earth wasn't yet done, and that God would rescue him from death at that point (Philippians 1:25). He didn't want to be prematurely ejected from this world, even though he himself suffered grief in many kinds of trials.

In talking about death, we need to seek to acquire the same balance that we see in the Bible. We don't embrace grief and pain but neither do we fear it as our ultimate enemy. Death is horrible. Death is defeated! Grief is real. So is grace. And the same God who has provided victory over death, will provide us with grace for life, even while we are going through grief.

Our final holiday with Michelle was a gift of grace. But it was also traumatic. We said goodbye, uncertain whether we would see her again. In under three months she did receive her full healing, although not in this life. So, we grieved deeply. But not without hope.

Ultimately, the hope we have is that God is in control, and that he has the whole world in his hands. This is the perspective we will explore in the next chapter.

REFLECT

I encourage you to take moments to reflect at the end of each chapter (and at times, during the chapters themselves).

As you reflect on this chapter, turn to Psalm 23. Perhaps view this visual version of the Psalm on the Grief and Grace website:

griefandgrace.org/the-lord-is-my-shepherd/

Ask the Lord Your Shepherd to walk with you as you read this book. Imagine that he is leading you beside green pastures and beside quiet waters.

Ask the Lord Your Shepherd to restore your soul.

Trust him to remove your fears and that he will comfort you as you continue to read this book.

CHAPTER TWO

WHO'S IN CHARGE ANYWAY?

He who has not eaten his bread in tears,
He who has not sat up weeping upon his bed
throughout the night of despair,
He knows you not, Oh Heavenly Father.
JOHAN WOLFGANG VAN GOETHE[6]

CHILDLIKE FAITH

What is your view of God? What words do you most often use to describe him? Do you think, live, and act with God in charge?

Our view of God will greatly impact our expectations of him when we encounter grief and death. In order to have a biblical perspective of death, we need to have a biblical perspective on the one who is the source of life.

I once again have a toddler in the home. Faith is twelve years younger than her sister. When her big sister was a toddler we didn't have uncapped internet, smart phones, or YouTube subscriptions. The world has changed. But then again, has it? Although we have all this new technology, we still access the same old TV programmes and kids songs that we played for all our older children when they were toddlers. Perhaps new technology just helps us become more nostalgic.

Faith is at a delightful age where life is just one big adventure and everything is new and exciting to her. She loves to sing and dance, so I try to find playlists of classic kids songs for her to dance and singalong to. One classic that has stood the test of time is 'He's Got the Whole World in His Hands'. The song explains that he's got animals, all of us, the tiny babies, *everything* in his hands. As Faith sings these words, she accepts them literally and has no reason to question their absolute truth.

I'm sure many of us sang this song as children. But has it just remained a child's song to us? As we've matured, become sophisticated, sought independence and developed scars from the hurt and pain that comes with the passage of time, do we still believe those words? More importantly, do we actively live those words out in the decisions we make, the actions we take and the attitudes we hold? As we consider our mortality and the mortality of those around us, do we still trust in the one who has the whole world in his hands?

WHO'S IN CHARGE?

Imagine a teenage party. The parents are away and while they are away, the kids will play. It gets past 10pm and the music is still pumping and the neighbours are beginning to be on edge. At 11pm, the volume goes up another level and by midnight the neighbours' patience is exhausted so they call the police. They arrive on the scene and bang on the front door. Above the din, a teenage voice calls, 'Who is it?' Someone has noticed that there are blue lights flashing on the driveway so they cut the music and turn out some lights. The police enter. As they shine their flashlights they ask the critical question: 'Who's in charge here?' A tentative teenage hand rises in the air. The officer looks and everything makes sense. He had intuitively realised that his question was a rhetorical one. The chaos has been caused because there is no appropriate authority present in the house, therefore there has been no boundary placed upon the youthful exuberance.

Now, I did have a few moments as a teenager that I won't share right now, but thankfully we never had the police come knocking on the front door. In our culture, authority can sometimes be portrayed with a negative connotation. We rebel against the idea of a coercive or controlling authority. However, this is not a biblical view of God's authority.

Rather, God's authority is one that ensures there is order rather than chaos. His authority is rooted in his love and his desire for us to live a full and joyous life. God took on flesh and came to earth because sin was robbing us of understanding our true purpose as it takes us outside the boundaries of God's loving authority. As Jesus explained, 'The thief comes only to steal and kill and destroy; I have come that they may have life, and have it to the full' (John 10:10).

When we exert our will over and above the will of God, it leads to chaos. When we surrender to his Lordship, what theologians call his sovereignty, then we find peace and joy. Let's consider this within the context of grief and loss.

I sometimes imagine how I might have responded to Laura's death if I didn't believe in the sovereignty of God. The reality is, I can't imagine it. I'm certain that my faith in God's sovereignty was an anchor that prevented me from completely falling to pieces. The hurt and pain were real and penetrated deeply into my soul. My heart ached and I longed not to have to walk the road of grief. I felt despair, loss, confusion and wept many tears of sorrow. Yet, deep within me, I knew I was not alone. Even in my loneliest moments in the months that followed, my faith rooted me in the knowledge that God was with me, that he cared for me, and that he was still in control. Even though I didn't feel happy about the situation I was in, I had a sense of deep assurance that I didn't need to answer all my own questions because I trusted in one who had the whole world, including Tim Tucker, in his hands.

You see, when theologians talk about the sovereignty of God, they are not simply talking about a doctrinal understanding of how awesome, powerful, and wise God is. It is not just a belief system that views God as the supreme ruler of the universe.[7] While those things are true, the sovereignty of God is a delightful theological truth because it has wonderful implications for us as his children. The Bible reveals that the perfect, eternal and sovereign Lord is intimately involved in all the details of my life and your life. Trusting in God's sovereignty means we believe that nothing happens in this world that is outside of God's plan for us and that he truly will work in all the events of our lives for our good and for his glory.[8] Sometimes, in the pain of life, we may strike out at God in anger because things haven't turned out the way we had hoped. And that's fine. I think God is big enough to cope with our outbursts. But, ultimately, we need to find our way back to Romans 8:28 – the classic go-to verse, which, if we really absorb it, should shape our perspective on everything that happens in this life, including our perspective on death: 'And we know that in all things God works for the good of those who love him, who have been called according to his purpose.'

REFLECT

I'm aware that we're treading on holy ground here. Before reading further in this chapter, I recommend you take some moments just to reflect.

Read Psalm 104 which beautifully and poetically depicts God as Lord over all creation.

Then turn back one page of your Bible (or swipe right on your digital device). Read Psalm 103 and see how David shows that the Lord of creation is intimately involved in the details of our lives. In particular, notice the following verses which show him as Lord of our life and of our death:

'As a father has compassion on his children, so the LORD has compassion on those who fear him; for he knows how we are formed, he remembers that we are dust. The life of mortals is like grass, they flourish like a flower of the field; the wind blows over it and it is gone and its place remembers it no more. But from everlasting to everlasting the LORD's love is with those who fear him, and his righteousness with their children's children – with those who keep his covenant and remember to obey his precepts.' – Psalm 103:13–18[9]

Now consider these questions:
– Do you really *believe* this?
– Do you *really* believe this?

CS Lewis wrote, 'You never know how much you really believe anything until its truth or falsehood becomes a matter of life and death to you.'[10]

Has your experience of death, grief or loss caused you to doubt God's sovereignty?

WHEN THE RUBBER HITS THE ROAD

Let me share two more examples of how critical this perspective is when we face griefs of many kinds. We'll start with a famous biblical example before jumping to the mid-20th Century.

I guess it's not a surprise that Job would feature in this book. It was not a matter of if, but when, this would be.

I'm sure you know the story. Job, a righteous man, is stripped of possessions, dignity, family and respect. Ultimately, the devil believes Job has a transactional faith. He'll follow God on condition that God preserves the status quo of his good life. God gives permission to Satan to test his thesis.[11] Following the demonic onslaught that ensues, Job's wife utters the words that are the logical conclusion of a transactional faith gone wrong: 'Curse God and die' (Job 2:9). But Job's faith is made of sterner stuff. His response:

> 'Naked I came from my mother's womb, and naked I will depart. The Lord gave and the Lord has taken away; may the name of the Lord be praised.' (Job 1:21)

Perhaps what's even more incredible is not just Job's words but his actions when uttering these words. Having torn his clothes (an ancient Middle Eastern symbol of grief and lament), he then 'fell to the ground in worship' (Job 1:20b). Clearly, Job is not happy about his material and physical demise. However, when the rubber hits the road, continuing to serve and worship God was his greatest priority, despite his circumstances. He was able to continue to worship God because he had the perspective that God was ultimately in charge.

Krish Kandiah writes:

'Job's confession reveals a commitment to continue trusting God despite his circumstances. Job's perspective is that life itself is a gift, and so is everything that comes with it, and he will continue to love God for who he is, not for what he has given to Job.'[12]

Kandiah goes on to say that the purpose of the whole book of Job is to teach us about God's sovereignty. 'In a book that addresses the problem of suffering there is no backing away from the fact that God is in control – there is no downplaying total divine sovereignty.'[13]

In fact, in 42 chapters, the book of Job does not explain why good people suffer. Rather, it shows that righteous people can still trust that God is in control and is working out his perfect purposes even in and through the difficulties we experience in life. All our questions may not be answered. But trusting in God's goodness enables us to find the strength to endure through tough times.

This leads to our second example. Martin Luther King was a primary leader in the 1960s civil rights movement in the United States. Committed to peaceful protest, King and his followers suffered hatred, persecution, violence and even death in the pursuit of equal rights for African Americans and other minorities. Amid this painful struggle, King had to find immense fortitude to not only remain committed to his non-violent stance but also to maintain the faith and courage of his followers. They needed consistent reassurance that, in spite of their immediate suffering, righteousness would ultimately overcome evil.

King's belief in God's sovereignty sustained him in the dark days that the civil rights movement experienced. Against the context of pain and struggle, King would quote these words from a poem by James Russell Lowell: 'behind the dim unknown, standeth God within the shadow, keeping watch above his own.'[14]

When the rubber hit the road, King's perspective of God's sovereignty was what sustained him, even when the risks were deadly. Philip Yancey helpfully explains the impact this had upon the civil rights activists:

'Already convinced of the justness of their cause, they wanted someone to lift their sights beyond the long string of disheartening failures. We now look back on the civil rights movement as a steady tidal surge towards victory. At the time, facing daily confrontations with the power structures and under constant intimidation from policemen, judges and even the FBI, civil rights workers had no assurance of victory. We forget how many nights they spent in rank Southern jails. Most of the time the present looked impossibly bleak, the future even bleaker... To such demoralised troops, King offered a vision of the world held in the hands of a just God… *For King, the long view meant remembering that, no matter how things appear at any given moment, God reigns.'*[15]

HIS WAYS ARE NOT OUR WAYS

As we have seen in these examples, when facing suffering, grief and death, there is a reality check we need to take. God's sovereignty is intrinsically linked to his infinite wisdom, which means there is much that God does which is beyond our comprehension. Therefore, our trust in him is not dependent upon our being able to understand and articulate the reason why God does things. In fact, it is just the opposite. Our trust in God is because we recognise his ways are beyond our understanding and his reasons beyond our comprehension. Yet we know that his ways and his reasoning are completely founded in his goodness, mercy and love. It is because of his character that we are able to trust him.

Isaiah 55:8–9 are famous verses that confirm that God's ways are on a completely different plane to ours:

"'For my thoughts are not your thoughts,
neither are your ways my ways,"
declares the Lord.
"As the heavens are higher than the earth,
    so are my ways higher than your ways
and my thoughts than your thoughts.'"

However, if we were uncertain of the character of God, then we would not find much comfort in these words. These verses in Isaiah follow God's promise that all those who come to him in repentance will find mercy (see 55:7). Isaiah asserts that God's ways are so completely different to ours because his character is always going to show mercy to the repentant, which is completely contrary to our human tendency. It is because of God's perfect and eternal character that we can trust him even when we don't understand his ways.

POWER AND LOVE

Psalm 62 was one of my go-to psalms during my period of deep grief. David gives us incredible assurance about the faithfulness of God as our rock, salvation, and the one in whom we can find rest and strength. But I particularly love the closing two verses:

> 'God has spoken once, Twice I have heard this: that power belongs to God. Also to you, O Lord, belong lovingkindness and compassion, For you compensate every man according to [the value of] his work.' (Psalm 62:11–12, AMP)

There are two critical truths that David affirms about the nature of God. Firstly, that God is *powerful*. He is all-powerful. This is the image of the creator and sustainer of the universe. The one who can perform miracles and has almighty strength. However, if all we knew about God was his power, then would we be able to trust him? What if he used his power against us or for nefarious ends? So, David secondly confirms that *lovingkindness and compassion* also belong to God. God's power is used in fundamental harmony with his love and compassion towards us. Imagine God had only love and compassion but no power? We'd maybe feel his sympathy but he'd have no ability to intervene in our situation.

Thankfully, the Bible reveals (and the testimony of millions through the ages confirms) that God is all-powerful and all-loving. These two qualities work in perfect unison for our good and his glory. This means we can trust in his sovereignty *even when we don't understand*.

It can feel risky and vulnerable to continue to have faith in God when we're facing life after the death of a loved one. David Platt helpfully writes:

> 'When we risk our lives to run after Christ we discover the safety that is found only in his sovereignty, the security that is found only in his love, and the satisfaction that is found only in his presence. This is the eternally great reward, and we would be foolish to settle for anything less.'[16]

As Platt demonstrates, our sense of assurance in God's sovereignty is intrinsically linked to the biblical perspective on eternity, which is the subject of the third chapter in this part of the book.

RESPOND

It's an incredible thought that Jesus also relied entirely on the sovereignty of God. Many of his prayers in the New Testament demonstrate this, most notably in the Garden of Gethsemane (see Luke 22:39–44).

Dallas Willard has written his interpretation of the prayer Jesus taught his disciples to pray. Read it carefully and note the reliance on God's sovereignty embodied in this prayer. Then adopt the prayer as your own and once again commit to surrender to God's sovereignty for your good and his glory.

'Dear Father always be near us,
may your name be treasured and loved,
may your rule be completed in us –
may your will be done here on earth
in just the way it is done in heaven.
Give us today the things we need today,
and forgive us our sins and impositions on you
as we are forgiving all who in any way offend us.
Please don't put us through trials,
but deliver us from everything bad.
Because you are the one in charge,
and you have all the power,
and the glory too is all yours – forever –
which is just the way we want it!'[17]

CHAPTER THREE

HEAVEN ON EARTH

Home is not a heavenly mansion in the afterlife but a
safe place right in the midst of our anxious world.
BRENNAN MANNING[18]

HYMN-SPIRATION

I grew up towards the end of the hymn book era. Let's conduct a quick recap of the past 50 years of technology in the church. Before smart screens we had digital projectors. Before digital projectors we had overhead projectors (OHPs). These were a technological disruptor that meant we could sing words from a screen rather than staring at a book. It required a relatively skilled operator who could face the slides the right way on the light screen and then manoeuvre the slide to make sure we were singing the right verse or the chorus.

And before OHPs we had hymn books. We'd enter church and be handed the hymn book. As we took our seats (or pews), we could check the morning's running order by looking at the hymn number board. We would then turn to the chosen hymn and stand to sing in unison to the accompaniment of a piano or organ. As we sang the hymns, I would often be distracted by two things. Firstly, the old-fashioned names of the hymn-writers. And, secondly, calculating the age at which they died and how old the hymns were, because the composer's birth and death dates were usually also included (unless it was anonymous).

Although hymn books are generally a thing of the past, have you ever marvelled at how some hymns stand the test of time? Songs that were written hundreds of years ago still provide spine-tingling moments of grand praise and worship. I don't think it's because we now have bigger musical productions, better sound systems or more creative arrangements. I rather feel it's because of the content of the hymns and the ageless theme of the lyrics.

This is what I've observed: all the hymns that remain as powerful now as the day they were written have an *eternal perspective*. Think about your favourite hymn, perhaps 'Amazing Grace', 'And Can It Be', or 'Be Thou My Vision'. All of these hymns take cognisance of the current troubles we might face as believers but then point us beyond the troubles to the assurance we have of eternity. They are signposts that we are on our way to a glorious future. While rooted in the reality of today, they provide a transcendent theme which gives us courage and hope for tomorrow.

The same can be said of the spiritual songs of the African American slaves which pointed the singers to the 'land beyond Jordan.'[19] As such, I feel I can also predict which of today's modern songs Christians will be singing in the coming centuries. For example, Matt Redman's immensely popular song '10,000 Reasons' concludes with this incredible verse:

> And on that day when my strength is failing,
> The end draws near and my time has come,
> Still my soul will sing your praise unending,
> Ten thousand years and then forevermore.

ETERNITY IN THE HUMAN HEART

I believe this heavenly perspective is one reason why the great Christian hymns and songs have been an incredible comfort to countless people who have endured grief. These songs resonate across decades and centuries because they remind us of a beautiful biblical truth. We are not finite beings. Though our flesh and blood will return to dust, our spirit is eternal and is created for life beyond the grave. When we accept Jesus as our Lord, our spirit is resurrected from death to life, and eternity is reignited in our souls.[20] The writer of Ecclesiastes wrote this intriguing verse,

> 'He has made everything beautiful in its time. He has also set eternity in the human heart; yet no one can fathom what God has done from beginning to end.' (Ecclesiastes 3:11)

Although we may not be able to fully fathom or comprehend the works of God from beginning to end, God has graciously placed a longing for eternity within our hearts. The arts are one vehicle through which we get foretastes of eternity while walking planet earth. I believe the greatest Christian hymns, songs and paintings help ignite that sense of eternity that has been placed within our hearts and cause us to long to know God better as we seek to live as citizens of heaven while still on earth.

START WITH THE END IN MIND

I'm sure, like me, you've said of someone that they are 'too heavenly minded for any earthly good'. We tend to reserve this judgement for people who have their 'head in the clouds' – they are dreamers, perhaps with a tendency to over-spiritualise things (we touched on this in chapter 1). The impression this gives is that to be 'heavenly-minded' is to be other-worldly, as if heaven has no relevance for this life. Heaven may be considered as a lofty ideal or concept that gives a sense of peace to those who are grieving. But thinking about heaven is considered by many to be, at best, a healthy distraction, and, at worst, a form of escapism or delusion that can cause us to become detached from reality.

I'd like to suggest that nothing can be further from the truth. I believe that a biblical view of heaven will enable us to become infinitely more useful on earth. Jesus, at the onset of his public ministry, proclaimed, 'Repent, for the kingdom of heaven has come near' (Matthew 4:17) and much of his teaching focused on what it means for his followers to be citizens of the kingdom of heaven while still living on earth.[21] He also taught his disciples to pray, 'Your kingdom come, your will be done, on earth as it is in heaven' (Matthew 6:10). Clearly, Jesus wasn't talking about heaven as a separate reality merely relevant for when we die. Rather, the kingdom of heaven is a realm that impacts the daily lives of God's followers who live under his Lordship as the sovereign king of heaven and earth.

In order for us to gain a biblical perspective that enables us to find life after death, it's important that we cultivate a heavenly perspective. My intention here is not to provide you with answers on what heaven is like.[22] My purpose is rather for us to consider what it means to already be heavenly citizens while we are still on earth. Heaven is not something simply for when we die. That perspective creates a false dichotomy between this life and the next life which you simply can't find in the Bible. No, when we become Christians our spirit is reborn and we begin eternal life immediately. As Paul tells us, 'Therefore, if anyone is in Christ, the new creation has come; the old has gone, the new is here' (2 Corinthians 5:17).

As a child of God, we enter into a new reality as a new person with a new identity and a new spiritual passport. The spiritual passport we've received supersedes our earthly passports and assures us that we are *already* citizens of the kingdom of heaven.

I believe this perspective, perhaps more than anything else, should help shape our counter-cultural view of death. This doesn't mean we're trying to create some kind of utopia or heaven on earth. That would contradict what we've already discovered about having to live in the realities of the consequences of sin and death. However, to enable us to face grief and loss with faith and hope, we need to start with the end in mind, recognising that our ultimate destiny is one of unimaginable peace and joy in the presence of God forever. Yet we are not to simply survive this 'dreadful' life until we enter heaven by the skin of our teeth! We should rather acknowledge that we are already citizens of heaven who are temporarily located on planet earth with a specific calling and mandate to be Christ's ambassadors until we die or Jesus returns (2 Corinthians 5:20).

WHAT WILL WE BE DOING IN TEN THOUSAND YEARS?

We're touching here on some critical matters which I know can be quite weighty and not always easy to understand. However, I believe that a heavenly perspective is an absolutely critical distinctive of the Christian faith and the source of our ultimate hope, not just for life beyond the grave, but for this life and particularly for life after the death of a loved one. So, let's turn to some incredible authors to help break it down further for us.

Dallas Willard (1935–2013) is one of my favourite American authors. He was a Christian philosopher and author.

In his book *The Divine Conspiracy*, he gives an insightful view on the continuity that exists for Christians between this life and the next. He explains that the eternal life which Jesus spoke about (as considered above), is primarily about our relationship with God. Willard states that eternal life is 'an intimately interactive relationship with him (God)'[23] which doesn't start when we die but starts the moment that we have faith in Jesus. He goes on to explain the assurance this brings as follows:

> '…we may be sure that our life – yes, that familiar one we are each so well acquainted with – will never stop. We should be anticipating what we will be doing three hundred or a thousand or ten thousand years from now in this marvellous universe.'[24]

This view is game-changing. Eternal life – communion with God – starts while we still live on earth. And our faith assures us that death is not a dangerous interruption but rather a conduit that enables us to continue our intimacy and communion with God for all eternity.

Randy Alcorn puts it this way: 'God and humanity will live together in eternal happiness, forever deepening their relationships, as the glory of God permeates every aspect of the new creation.'[25]

This is what we mean by having an eternal perspective. Andy Hawthorne, Founder and Global CEO of The Message Trust (my boss!) states that Paul's greatest asset was that he had a heavenly perspective.[26] His eternal perspective motivated him to pursue Christ (Philippians 1:21), preach to unbelievers (1 Corinthians 9:27), and persevere through hardship (2 Corinthians 4:16–18). As another author, NT Wright said: '"Our citizenship is in heaven"; yes, but that is the model and type for your citizenship upon earth.'[27]

I hope you can agree that the Bible makes it clear that having an eternal/heavenly perspective is not 'pie in the sky when we die' but critically relevant to our day-to-day lives. Having the assurance of eternity enables us to live in the present in a counter-cultural way. Dane Ortlund helpfully summarises the implications: 'We will be less sinful in the next life than we are now, but we will not be any more secure in the next life than we are now.'[28]

This helps us understand what John teaches about loving this world:

'Do not love the world or anything in the world. If anyone loves the world, love for the Father is not in them. For everything in the world – the lust of the flesh, the lust of the eyes, and the pride of life – comes not from the Father but from the world. The world and its desires pass away, but whoever does the will of God lives forever.' (1 John 2:15–17)

We don't need to be consumed with love for this life because we know that this is just a foretaste of what is in store for us.

WE HAVE ALREADY DIED

In fact, we can take our biblical perspective one step further. Our security as Christians and the continuity between this life and the next is ultimately due to the fact that we are already dead. Paul makes this abundantly clear:

> I have been crucified with Christ and I no longer live, but Christ lives in me. The life I now live in the body, I live by faith in the Son of God, who loved me and gave himself for me." (Galatians 2:20)

A friend of mine says, 'I'm already dead – so what's the worst that can happen?' When we became Christians we didn't just receive a makeover. No, we died! And we were resurrected. Dallas Willard quotes the great 19th Century Christian and humanitarian, George Mueller:

> 'There was a day when I died: died to George Mueller, his opinions, preferences, tastes and will; died to the world, its approval or censure; died to the approval or blame even of my brethren or friends, and since then I have studied only to show myself "approved unto God."'[29]

Understanding that we're already dead and that we have been set free from our slavery to sin and self, is extremely liberating and changes our outlook on everything. We need to start viewing this life through our resurrected eyes. This viewpoint is the faith-life that enables us to walk by faith rather than by sight (see 2 Corinthians 5:7), and it changes everything.

The 20th Century Chinese pastor, church planter and author, Watchman Nee wrote:

'If I believe in the death of the Lord Jesus, then I can believe in my own death just as surely as I believe in his… Let me tell you. *You have died!* You are done with! You are ruled out! The self you loathe is on the Cross in Christ. And "he that is dead is freed from sin" (Romans 6:7). This is the Gospel for Christians.'[30]

FALLING ASLEEP

I hope I haven't lost you as I've reeled off all those quotes. However, I feel it's important that we recognise the consistent teaching of Christians from different eras and contexts. Clearly, this is a subject that could consume a whole book and it's important that we keep the main thing, the main thing in this particular book. The critical point I want us to understand is that, because of the resurrection life that saves us from sin and death, there is continuity between this life and the next, rather than discontinuity. If we can comprehend this, then it will help shape the way we grieve as believers, particularly as we grieve for those who knew Jesus.

This is why the biblical writers talk of death as 'falling asleep'. When we die, we close our eyes to this world and awaken in the presence of Jesus. Paul wrote this verse to encourage the church in Thessalonica:

'Brothers and sisters, we do not want you to be uninformed about those who sleep in death, so that you do not grieve like the rest of mankind, who have no hope.'
(1 Thessalonians 4:13)

On 18 August 2016, I watched Laura's last breaths after the doctors switched off her life support machine. I watched her physical body die. But I believe that as she went to sleep for the last time on earth, she awoke in eternity and was more alive than ever before. I believe that heaven would not have felt a strange place to her and she was certainly no stranger there. She stepped into the life she had been prepared for. She was now in a place without evil, pain and suffering and I'm sure that caused her spirit to rejoice as her voice joined with the songs of angels in praise and worship of Jesus.

Randy Alcorn says: 'To see God will be our greatest joy. Not only will we see his face and live – we will likely wonder if we ever lived before we saw his face.'[31]

With this knowledge, how can I then grieve like the rest of mankind? Notice that Paul doesn't say we mustn't grieve, but that we grieve with hope, with the assurance that there is life after death, both for those who die as believers and for those who remain behind.

WHAT ABOUT THOSE WHO DON'T BELIEVE?

It would be remiss of me not to give a thought to those of us who have grieved the loss of unbelievers. Life after the death of someone who is not a believer is particularly difficult. Although God's grace is available to all and his desire is for all to be saved (1 Timothy 2:4), there are still millions of people who die having not chosen to surrender their lives to Christ.

Those who grieve the loss of an unbeliever are faced with the reality that they may never see that person again. It is actually cruel to try and pretend otherwise when the scriptures are so clear. It would not be kind of me to offer false hope in this regard when Jesus was clear in his teaching that those who do not repent and believe will be banished from God's presence. He spoke of hell as a real place and we deny the gospel if we modify the Bible's teaching.[32] However, knowing this can cause a double measure of grief and sadness for a mourning believer after the death of an unbelieving family member or friend.

Clearly, we do not know the work that God does in the heart of someone in the moments before they die. There are many examples of last-minute grace, ever since the man on the cross next to Jesus cried out for salvation (Luke 23:40–43). My own grandmother surrendered her life to Jesus in the final few days of her life. One of my longest standing and best friends recommitted his life to God in the final month of his life. Conversely, my grandfather died without us having any reasonable assurance that he had come to a place of repentance and faith in Jesus. There is no simple answer or solution for how to handle these tough situations. It is a difficult road to walk when there is no guarantee that someone we love is resting in peace. However, we must, like Abraham, recognise that the Judge of all the earth will do what is right (Genesis 18:25). Indeed, as we have noted before, we trust the sovereignty of God, not because we understand his ways, but because his plans and purposes far exceed ours.

My main advice here is that we should not try to sugar-coat something that Jesus didn't. Our testimony to the world is at stake and we need to be consistent in our application of scripture. Yet, this should never be in a judgemental or condemnatory fashion. When we speak of the death of someone who was not a Christian, we need to be particularly compassionate to those who are grieving and once again remind ourselves of our utter dependence upon the grace of God. Additionally, understanding God's sovereignty means that mourning believers should not carry guilty feelings of, 'could I have done more?' or 'did I miss opportunities?' etc. It is critical that a community of people support those going through this double grief, providing comfort and love during an extremely difficult season of their lives.

Given these difficult realities, we also need once again to be cognisant of the calling that is upon us as believers to be witnesses to the life, death and resurrection of Christ. We live in a hurting world where billions of people are still living without the assurance that they are going to heaven. As Paul wrote, let's make the most of every opportunity to share about the hope that we have in order that many more people will come to know the love, grace, mercy and compassion of God (Colossians 4:5–6). A measure of healing can come as we see others begin experiencing the joy of being a citizen of heaven while they are still on earth.

LIGHT AND MOMENTARY STRUGGLES

We have spent three chapters considering a biblical perspective on life after the death of a loved one. Having a biblical perspective transforms how we view death and enables us to find the grace and strength to continue serving Christ even as we journey through grief. As we've already seen, Paul is an incredible example of someone who had a heavenly perspective and this dictated how he viewed life.

In his second letter to the church in Corinth, Paul spells out to them the challenges he was facing as an apostle. Day and night his life was under threat. He had experienced incredible suffering and was being persecuted. In 2 Corinthians 11, Paul lists what he has endured in his service of Christ including beatings, stonings, being ship-wrecked and left for dead many times.

Yet, in 2 Corinthians 2 he says these incredible words:

'Therefore we do not lose heart. Though outwardly we are wasting away, yet inwardly we are being renewed day by day. For our light and momentary troubles are achieving for us an eternal glory that far outweighs them all. So we fix our eyes not on what is seen, but on what is unseen. For what is seen is temporary, but what is unseen is eternal.' (2 Corinthians 2:16–18)

Paul (as usual) has hit the nail on the head. When we have an eternal perspective, it changes everything. As we've seen above, when our minds are considering what our life will be like ten thousand years from now, then our current challenges are seen as 'light and momentary troubles'. Having that eternal perspective enables us to face tomorrow, as hard as that might immediately seem.

Having a biblical perspective, however, does not mean we are immune to pain. Having laid a foundation in biblical truth, the next three chapters will consider how we respond to the pain that the death of a loved one causes us.

REFLECT

'When you hear these huge hymns, you can survive any loss. You can take any amount of blows. You can make the most difficult decisions. You can march forward in your life against all adversity.'[33]

To conclude this part on perspective, spend some time reflecting on the lyrics of the three hymns I mentioned previously (I have included some of the key verses below). Perhaps listen to them on YouTube or Spotify and meditate on the words, particularly as they point you beyond the pain of this life and lead you into the eternal presence of our Lord and Saviour. Let the eternal truths speak to your soul.

'And Can It Be' (Charles Wesley, 1738)

Long my imprisoned spirit lay
Fast bound in sin and nature's night;
Thine eye diffused a quick'ning ray,
I woke, the dungeon flamed with light;
My chains fell off, my heart was free;
I rose, went forth and followed Thee.

No condemnation now I dread;
Jesus, and all in Him is mine!
Alive in Him, my living Head,
And clothed in righteousness divine,
Bold I approach th'eternal throne,
And claim the crown, through Christ my own.

'Be Thou My Vision' (Eleanor Hull, 1912)

Riches I heed not, nor vain, empty praise
Thou mine inheritance, now and always

Thou and Thou only first in my heart
High King of heaven, my treasure Thou art.

High King of heaven, my victory won
May I reach heaven's joys, O bright heaven's sun
Heart of my own heart, whatever befall
Still be my vision, O ruler of all.

'Amazing Grace' (John Newton, 1779)

Through many dangers, toils, and snares
I have already come
This grace that brought me safe thus far
And grace will lead me home.

When we've been there ten thousand years
Bright, shining as the sun
We've no less days to sing God's praise
Than when we first begun.

Amazing grace how sweet the sound
That saved a wretch like me
I once was lost, but now I'm found
Was blind but now I see.

PART TWO

PAIN

CHAPTER FOUR

THE STING OF DEATH

I felt as if my soul were being torn from my
body when I saw his life depart.
TERESA OF AVILA[34]

CONSUMED BY ANGUISH

The previous three chapters have helped provide a biblical perspective on life after death. I realise that I've run the risk in opening the book with these chapters of not fully acknowledging the depth of suffering associated with 'grief of many kinds' (1 Peter 1:6). Just because Christians have a different perspective doesn't mean that they have a different tolerance level to pain. As we'll see in the next three chapters, Christian believers are not immune from the pain of grief. Life after the death of a loved one is terribly painful. The Bible is realistic about this and the Bible shows that healing doesn't come by ignoring the pain, imagining it isn't there, or any other 'mind over matter' tricks that we might employ. The Bible shows that pain must be faced if we are to find healing.

The perspective we've gained in the previous three chapters gives us a horizon that we must keep in view when we are bereaved. However, we still need to walk through the valley of the shadow of death. That's the journey we'll be taking in these next three chapters.

As we have seen, the Bible is not shy to talk about death. Yet the Bible doesn't predominantly approach the subject of death from a theoretical or philosophical perspective. Rather, many of the biblical passages concerning death are deeply emotional as the authors face the reality of pain, grief and loss. Death is presented as a nefarious enemy entirely at odds with God's plans and purposes. Many of the psalms grapple with our vulnerability as mortal humans living in the shadow of death. David, in Psalm 31, gives expression to the human experience in very graphic language:

> 'Be merciful to me, Lord, for I am in distress; my eyes grow weak with sorrow, my soul and body with grief. My life is consumed by anguish and my years by groaning; my strength fails because of my affliction, and my bones grow weak.' (Psalm 31:9–13)

The Message translation of the same verses is as follows:

> 'Be kind to me, God – I'm in deep, deep trouble again. I've cried my eyes out; I feel hollow inside. My life

leaks away, groan by groan; my years fade out in sighs. My troubles have worn me out, turned my bones to powder.' (Psalm 31:9–10, MSG)

Aren't these descriptions akin to what we might today call depression? David is face to face with his mortality and is in distress, consumed by anguish and in great suffering.

Can you identify with David's words? Is it comforting to read that the great biblical characters also felt the sting of death? I imagine that anyone who has faced long-term illness or seen the demise of a loved one can relate to this language.

However, given the perspective we've considered in the first three chapters of this book, we might ask why David's language is not more triumphal. Why is he not facing death with more hope? Some might argue that this is the Old Testament and David would have responded differently if he had the New Testament perspective that we considered in the first three chapters of this book. Perhaps his response to pain and loss was because he didn't have a developed theology of suffering as he lived before Christ's victory on the cross. Maybe how Christians experience grief and loss should be different after the life, death and resurrection of Christ? Given the perspective we've explored, are we meant to be thick-skinned, full of hope and less prone to depression? Is it a denial of our faith to feel sad and lonely when we face grief of many kinds? Is there some kind of immunity to pain that Christians should have when facing life after the death of a loved one? Should our experience of grief be different now we're living beyond the resurrection of Jesus?

TRAGEDY STRIKES THE EARLY CHURCH

In considering these questions, I've found the example of the early church extremely helpful. Just a few years after Jesus' ascension, the church in Jerusalem faced an incredible challenge as one of their bright young leaders was stoned to death.

Stephen is the first recorded martyr in the New Testament church. Two chapters of Luke's account of the Acts of the Apostles are given to Stephen's last moments on earth (Acts 6 and 7). And twice in the space of a few verses Stephen is recommended to us in glowing terms. As one of the seven emerging leaders appointed to serve within the growing church, Luke says he was a man full of faith, grace, and power. Filled with the Spirit, he performed many miraculous signs (see Acts 6:5, 8). It was the public nature of his ministry that provoked opposition which escalated into an out and out confrontation with the Jewish leaders. Stephen was seized and brought in front of the Sanhedrin, the Jewish religious court.

Following the statements of various false witnesses, Stephen is given an opportunity to defend himself. He takes the opportunity to preach the gospel, demonstrating its continuity with the Jewish scriptures and culminating in calling out these Jewish leaders for their hypocrisy. This was the proverbial red flag to the bull. The angry mob convict Stephen of blasphemy and commence stoning him to death. As the rocks are raining down on him, Stephen utters the incredible words that have served for two millennia as a model of faith in the face of the worst that the devil and the world can throw at us. As they cast their stones, he prayed 'Lord Jesus, receive my spirit' and then, remarkably, follows the example of his Lord by also praying that God would forgive his persecutors (Acts 7:59–60). Then, he died.

What do we make of this story? Clearly, this was a significant moment in the life of the early church. Stephen is the first follower of Jesus to die as a direct result of his faith. There are many things we can note as we reflect on this story. Stephen was young and had the reputation of being a good man. He did nothing deserving of death. Many would see this a tragedy; the death of a newly elected leader with his best years still in front of him. Such a waste! Most importantly we observe that God does not intervene, at least, not in the way we might hope or expect. There were a myriad of ways that God could have rescued Stephen, such as his rescue of Shadrach, Meshach and Abednego from Nebuchadnezzar's furnace (see Daniel 3:16–28). Perhaps what could be considered more perplexing is that God was clearly present but rather than rescuing Stephen, he gives him a vision of Jesus. In the final moments of his life, Stephen sees the resurrected Jesus alive and well, in the heavenlies at the right hand of God (Acts 7:56).

So, is this purely a heroic story of how one man overcame the sting of death in a glorious way? We've already seen in this book that the Old Testament was realistic about death and the

pain it causes. However, in the light of Jesus' death and resurrection, are we now more immune to the pain of death? Is
the assurance of faith grounds to actually celebrate the death
of believers? Was there a seismic shift after Jesus that meant
that grieving is not relevant or necessary anymore? If so, then
wouldn't we expect the early church to have celebrated Stephen's
death as a great victory of a suffering saint?

STEPHEN'S FRIENDS

Through the course of my life, I've read this story many times
and it was only when I was reading it through the lens of my
own grief that I noticed one little verse in a fresh light. In
chapter 8, Luke records that the dam walls burst and persecution broke out widely against the early church, largely instigated
by Saul. The man who would become Paul and the greatest
church planter in history, was seeking to destroy the church
(Acts 8:3). This led to a scattering of God's people who escaped
from Jerusalem but then took the gospel message wherever
they went. However, before Luke begins to describe the impact
of the scattering, he records this short, but helpful, postscript
on Stephen's story: 'Godly men buried Stephen and mourned
deeply for him' (Acts 8:2).

I find this incredibly helpful. The Bible demonstrates that
death still hurts. Life after the loss of a loved one still stings.
Even though Stephen's friends, as godly people, would have had
a biblical perspective on death and would have believed he was

with Jesus, free of pain and suffering, they still mourned deeply for him.

Let's underline the logical conclusion. Mourning, grief, sadness and even depressive feelings are ok in the light of the death of someone we love. In fact, godly people *will* mourn. Stephen's friends mourned deeply. A more literal translation of the Greek is that these devout men 'made great lamentation over him'. The picture I get from this is of people in deep emotional turmoil, devastated at the loss of their friend. Just as being a Christian hadn't made Stephen immune from suffering, so the early church community did not bypass the pain of grief after his death.

Stephen's story reveals the paradox of being a Christian. He approached death with the assurance that this life was a temporary sojourn and he would soon be with Jesus. Yet he still suffered! Those rocks battered and bruised him till his life gave way. God didn't give Stephen a route to bypass the pain of death. And it's the same for his friends. Even though they had assurance that he was now with Jesus, they felt his loss deeply. It hurt! And they had to learn to continue with their lives with the pain of that loss. This is the reality of life after the death of a loved one.

DEATH IS PAINFUL

So, this chapter has one main point. Death is painful for those that remain. No matter how we try to explain it, rationalise it or theologise about it, death is painful. And the counsel the Bible provides is that mourning is a righteous and necessary response to death. The godly men who buried Stephen give us all liberty not to repress our feelings but to lament deeply over those we've lost. 'Lament is the honest cry of a hurting heart wrestling with the paradox of pain and the promise of God's goodness.'[35]

CS Lewis, reflecting on the loss of his wife, wrote the following:

> 'Bereavement is a universal and integral part of our experience of love. It follows marriage as normally as marriage follows courtship or as autumn follows summer. It is not a truncation of the process but one of its phases; not the interruption of the dance but the next figure.'[36]

The truth is, Christians *should* grieve. As Lewis said, bereavement is natural and it's also necessary. Death brings pain and pain cannot be ignored. The Bible doesn't teach that grieving is inappropriate for Christians. Even when it says 'we do not grieve' like the rest of mankind (1 Thessalonians 4:13), it is not denying that we should mourn, rather, in our bereavement we are not hope-less.

When we see a brother or sister grieving loss and in pain, we should mourn with them. Our role is not to try to be motivators to help them see the bright side. In the aftermath of a traumatic event, it is not helpful to say things like, 'at least you know where they are.' Although this may be theologically accurate, it is completely insensitive. To mourn with someone, we need to ask God to give us a gift of empathy. When Job went through his terrible ordeal, three of his friends decided to go and be with him. Job 2:11–13 gives a great model for how we can empathetically share in someone's suffering:

> 'When they saw him from a distance, they could hardly recognize him; they began to weep aloud, and they tore their robes and sprinkled dust on their heads. Then they sat on the ground with him for seven days and seven nights. No one said a word to him, because they saw how great his suffering was.'

The depth of their empathy is striking. They *wept aloud*. I grew up in the UK where death is treated in hushed tones and funerals are very sombre, silent affairs. You may hear the odd sniffle, but most Brits try to keep a stiff upper lip. I've lived most of my adult life in South Africa and travelled extensively to other African countries. The contrast is striking. In Africa grief is generally expressed by loud weeping, wailing and many tears. The relatives and wider community share in this public expression of pain. I can't help but feel this is a healthier cultural expression than my own background.

It was unfortunate that Job's friends moved from this posture of empathy to one where they felt that they needed to explain why Job was suffering. Their theological framework meant that the only reasonable explanation they could find was that Job had brought this on himself because of some deep-seated sinfulness. Clearly, not only was this unhelpful to Job in his pain but it was also rejected outrightly by God (see Job 42:7). Let's seek to follow their initial example of silently suffering alongside a grieving person rather than seeking to give theological explanations while they are in deep grief.

IT HURTS

Life after the death of a loved one is tough. One of the best descriptions of grief that I've come across is by Michelle Obama in her autobiography, *Becoming*. She wrote the following to describe life after the death of her father:

> 'It hurts to live after someone has died. It just does. It can hurt to walk down a hallway or open the fridge. It hurts to put on a pair of socks, to brush your teeth. Food tastes like nothing. Colours go flat. Music hurts, and so do memories. You look at something you'd otherwise find beautiful – a purple sky at sunset or a playground full of kids – and it only somehow deepens the loss. Grief is so lonely this way.'[37]

If you are currently grieving the loss of a loved one, or have ever experienced the emotional weight of bereavement, then I'm sure you can relate to what Obama has written. I've also been there. I've described in *Grief and Grace* how, in the months after Laura's death, time seemed to slow down. It's like life went into slow motion. A minute seemed like an hour, an hour like a day, and a day like a week. It was exhausting and just doing normal daily tasks drained my emotional strength. I'm so sorry if this is what you are experiencing right now. Death has a sting and we need to give ourselves permission to grieve. There is no recipe to recovery, no fast track, no simple 'getting over it'. Rather, it is a step-by-step process that requires patience and perseverance.

WORKING THROUGH GRIEF

Author and psychologist, Dr Henry Cloud, writes, 'The truth is that to the degree we were invested in something that's ending, we will have to work the grief through our system in order to be ready for whatever is next.'[38]

In his book *Necessary Endings*, Dr Cloud applies this to all loss we may experience in our lives. So, if that's true of the loss of a job, a change in our circumstances, a relocation etc. how much truer is it of the loss of someone we love. We cannot, we should not, seek to ignore or bypass the critically important process of grief. For as long as it takes, it needs to be worked through. God has designed us that way.

Some people might say to you, 'it takes time, but you will get over it.' My experience is that when someone you have loved dies, you never really 'get over it'. I don't think that is helpful language. As we will see later in this book, and as Dr Cloud alludes to, there is a *next* that we can discover. However, grief has different phases and different shades. I prefer to say that it's not something you get over, but grief is something you will continue to journey through. And that's a healthy thing.

Like Stephen's friends, we can make great lamentation over those we've lost as we navigate this difficult life. Yet, in that place of deep suffering, we can also experience fresh understanding about the depth of God's love, which we'll consider further in the next chapter.

REFLECT

Mark Vroegop has written a very helpful book called *Dark Clouds, Deep Mercy: Discovering the Grace of Lament*.

He provides a biblical framework to help us lament. He says: 'Lament is how you live between a hard life and God's promises. It is how we learn to sing and worship when suffering comes our way.'[39]

In the appendix to this book, Vroegop lists 29 Psalms of lament. Indeed, five of the first ten Psalms are laments: Psalm 3, 4, 5, 7 and 10.

Choose one of these Psalms and consider:
– How does the psalmist present his complaint to God?
– What did the psalmist ask of God in his prayer?

– How did the psalmist demonstrate their trust in God in spite of their situation?

Now consider your own situation. Is there a lament you need to bring before God?

– Bring your complaint before God. Honestly bare your heart to him.
– What are you asking of God? What is your humble request of him?
– Declare your trust in God in spite of your circumstances.

This is not a quick fix solution but can become a pattern to help you lament pain and walk through grief in a God-honouring way.

Before moving on to the next chapter, watch this short video on the Grief and Grace website:

griefandgrace.org/walking-with-grief/

CHAPTER FIVE

DEEP CRIES OUT TO DEEP

We are far beyond our depth when we come to the ocean
of divine purposes. We may gaze into the mystery with
awe, but to profess to comprehend it is vanity itself.
CH SPURGEON[40]

GOOD PEOPLE SUFFER

In January 2020, I had my first video chat with Raymond Bukenya. Raymond is a Christian minister in Uganda whose wife had died in April 2019 aged just 33, leaving him a young widower with three small children. Brenda had passed following a short battle with cancer. Given the similarity in our experiences, a mutual friend had given Raymond a copy of *Grief and Grace* and also introduced us to one another. We agreed to keep in touch and talk regularly.

Strangely though, after our initial conversation in January 2020, I didn't hear from Raymond for some time. I wondered why he didn't respond to my messages until I eventually got a call from him a few weeks later explaining the reason for his silence.

On 28 January, Raymond was riding his motorbike on the busy streets of Kampala. He doesn't remember exactly how the accident happened, other than a car was trying to overtake him and it eventually attempted a dangerous manoeuvre which resulted in the collision with Raymond. The actual details are sketchy. What is known is that Raymond was soon in hospital, fighting for his life. He underwent two major operations on his left lung and lower jaw. He had a fractured clavicle, scapula and rib. And then, six weeks later, upon leaving hospital, it was discovered he had long-term nerve damage on his left side that has left him with a non-functional left arm and consistent neuropathic pain.[41]

I remember first hearing the news and thinking, 'Lord, has this man not been through enough already?' It naturally begs the question, why do some people seem to experience such deep suffering while other people apparently breeze through life? And why is some of the worst suffering meted out on those who are seeking to follow Christ and live a godly life?

This is the question that Asaph had. He was the author of Psalm 73 who nearly lost his faith because he observed that righteous people suffered while evil people thrived (Psalm 73:2–3). This Psalm first impacted me when I was suffering from chronic fatigue syndrome as a young adult. I had been chronically unwell for 18 months. My life was on pause and I was grappling with the familiar questions around God's purpose in suffering and why he allows 'good' people to go through difficult times. The interesting thing about Asaph is that he never received an answer to this challenging question. However, his outlook changed when he 'entered the sanctuary of God' (Psalm 73:17). When Asaph spent time in God's presence he received a deeper revelation of who God is, which altered his perspective and enabled him to pen these incredible words:

'Whom have I in heaven but you?
And earth has nothing I desire besides you.
My flesh and my heart may fail,
but God is the strength of my heart
and my portion for ever.' (Psalm 73:25–26)

Raymond had suffered deeply. At the time of his motorbike accident, he was still grieving and adjusting to life after the death of his wife. While in hospital, not only was he having to cope with intense physical pain but he was also fearful for his children. Would they now lose their father so soon after the loss of their mother? Even if he didn't die, would he be well enough to care for them?

Over the next three years, Raymond would continue to reflect on the nature of suffering, while continuing to face grave difficulties in his personal and professional circumstances in the aftermath of these two seismic moments of his life.

Raymond has written a thesis on suffering drawing on research he's conducted with a rural Ugandan tribe and also reflecting on his personal experience. As with Asaph (and Job,

David and Stephen's friends), his master's thesis doesn't explain *why* God allows his children to suffer. He rather describes how suffering is an opportunity to follow Jesus more deeply. He writes: 'Suffering is a fact of life for the whole creation. All creatures suffer and die. The disciples of Jesus Christ are not exempted from suffering and death. Rather, they are called to follow Jesus in this world of suffering.'[42]

MOVING OUT OF THE SHALLOWS

Raymond's example is a spiritually mature response to suffering. His response has come as he has grappled with his devastating experiences in the light of his faith in God and the revelation of the Bible. This is not an easy thing to do. But engaging with the difficulties of life in this way ensures we avoid the pitfalls of making shallow responses to suffering and enables us to enter into a deeper relationship with God. The reality is we can become overwhelmed as we get plunged more deeply into an ocean of grief. However, once again, the Bible is our guide to finding hope even when the pain of loss threatens to consume us.

The sons of Korah wrote Psalm 42 which opens with the famous line, 'As the deer pants for the water so my soul pants for you, my God' (Psalm 42:1).

These words are familiar to us because we sing them to a soothingly melodic tranquil melody (perhaps, like me, it plays in your mind as you read the verses). This might conjure up an image of a peaceful scene as a cute deer gently laps up some water. However, the reality is that this is a deer that is running for its life. It is desperately seeking to escape the hunter and is in danger of dying of thirst while being pursued. It doesn't merely want to sip water while gently resting by an enchanting stream. No, it needs to drink to survive.

Grief can be dangerous territory for our faith. We may relate to that deer, which is being hunted down. It is petrified and disorientated. Psalm 42 is a psalm written for those who are in the depths of despair. Just as a deer is desperate for water to survive while being pursued by a predator, so the psalmist is thirsting for God while going through spiritual turmoil. They feel detached and isolated from God's presence which causes them to be plunged into a deep depression.[43]

As we've seen previously, the Bible is not scared to face the realities of pain; the depression, confusion and feelings of abandonment that it can cause. The word the psalmist uses to describe their emotional state is 'downcast' (Psalm 42:5, 11). Synonyms for downcast are sad, dejected, pessimistic, disap-pointed. There is no superficiality here. There is brutal honesty before God. They go on to write,

'I say to God my Rock, "Why have you forgotten me? Why must I go about mourning, oppressed by the enemy?" My bones suffer mortal agony as my foes taunt me, saying to me all day long, "Where is your God?"' (Psalm 42:9–10)

Even in this place of mortal spiritual danger, the psalmist musters up a modicum of faith. In my imagination they say these words through gritted teeth,

> 'Why, my soul, are you downcast? Why so disturbed within me? Put your hope in God, for I will yet praise him my Saviour and my God.' (Psalm 42:5, 11)

How do they do this? How do they manage to still find faith in God in spite of fear, loneliness and pain. I feel the clue is in verse 7. The psalmist has discovered something profound which I believe can help all of us hold on to our faith through times of immense pain.

> 'Deep calls out to deep in the roar of your waterfalls, all your waves and breakers have swept over me.' (Psalm 42:7)

From the depths of despair, they cry out to God and discover that God is there in the deep waters. As we learned about God's sovereignty in chapter 2, so we see the application of his sovereignty here. Not only is God in charge in a macro, universal sense. God is also involved in a micro and intimate sense. He is in the waves, the breakers and the depths. As we've seen in other scriptures, Psalm 42 does not attempt to give a reason for the suffering the author is experiencing. Rather, they discover that, right there in the deep waters of their most painful trials, God is with them. In the deep waters of their pain, they cry out to God and find that God is also the God of the depths.[44]

No matter how deep our painful experience, the love of God is deeper still and the psalmist exhorts us to hang on to hope in God at all costs. Elizabeth Elliot, twice widowed within twenty years, writes, 'it's through the deepest suffering that God has taught me the deepest lessons.'[45]

MAN OF SORROWS

A critical lesson we discover as we encounter painful trials, is not only that God sympathises with us when we are suffering (this in itself would be remarkable given that most ancient gods were depicted as aloof and unconcerned about human pain), but also that through our pain we can gain a deeper understanding that God himself suffers. The depth of our suffering is surpassed by the depths into which God has suffered in order to show us his redeeming love.

The central character of Isaiah 40 to 53 is a servant who has been appointed by God. Throughout these chapters, the characteristics and vocation of the servant is increasingly revealed. At his core, the servant of God is a suffering servant who endures intense pain in order to bring redemption to others.[46] Isaiah 53 is the climax of this passage, containing vivid descriptions of the suffering that God's chosen servant would endure.

The following verses are very familiar. Try to read them afresh and allow the wonder and horror of what the suffering servant endured penetrate your soul:

'He was despised and rejected by mankind, a man of suffering, and familiar with pain. Like one from whom people hide their faces he was despised, and we held him in low esteem.

'Surely he took up our pain and bore our suffering, yet we considered him punished by God, stricken by him, and afflicted.

'But he was pierced for our transgressions, he was crushed for our iniquities, the punishment that brought us peace was on him, and by his wounds we are healed.' (Isaiah 53:3–5)

We know, from the vantage point of the New Testament, that this is a prophecy about Jesus, the Son of God.[47] He was the suffering servant. He endured what was prophesied in this passage and secured for us the benefits of redemption as a result of his obedience. Consider the implications of this. When we cry out in the depths of our pain, we do not cry to a God who is merely sympathetic, rather we cry out to one who is familiar with suffering. Dane Ortlund writes:

'Contrary to what we expect to be the case, therefore, the deeper into weakness and suffering and testing we go, the deeper Christ's solidarity with us. As we go down into pain and anguish, we are descending ever deeper *into* Christ's very heart, not away from it.'[48]

CHRIST'S SOLIDARITY WITH US

Those words of Ortlund are remarkable. The assurance we have when we go through grief is that Jesus Christ, the Son of God, is the companion who understands the depth of our pain. The cross is the ultimate fulfilment of Isaiah's prophecy. Jesus endured the most painful execution invented by humans while God the Father endured the pain of seeing his son carry our sin.

The cross was the culmination of Jesus' life in which he shared the grief and sorrow which are common to all humans. Christ's solidarity with us is further revealed when we consider the breadth of human sorrow that he experienced over the course of his relatively short life.

The Son of God was born into poverty and raised in obscurity. As an infant, his family had to escape being hunted down by a tyrant. They adapted to life as refugees in Egypt for almost four years. As a young man, Jesus' earthly father died. He must have grieved deeply for Joseph. I'm sure Jesus greatly loved and admired Joseph who displayed the godly characteristics of humility, faith and obedience, even at the risk of his own reputation. Joseph raised Jesus to be a faithful Jew and apprenticed him as a carpenter. Although the Bible is silent about his death, we can only imagine that his loss deeply impacted Jesus.

We often focus on the high points of Jesus' public ministry, of which there were many incredible moments recorded in the gospels. However, alongside his growing popularity, he experienced mounting opposition. He was rejected in his hometown. His life was constantly under threat and he was always on the move. He had no permanent home and had to carefully navigate his movements, depending entirely on the guidance of the Holy Spirit and his communion with the Father. His enemies publicly accused him while they privately plotted against him. And the ultimate enemy, Satan, tempted him to bypass all the suffering by offering him an easier route to greatness. But Jesus knew the fickleness of popularity as the same people who had celebrated his arrival to Jerusalem with singing and palm leaves, just a few days later were shouting 'crucify him'.

Jesus also experienced the vulnerability of intimate friendships and that the wounds caused by those closest to us normally cut deepest. He was misunderstood by his family. He was rejected many times by individuals who came to him for help. He was also rejected by groups of people who had initially followed him and there is a deep sense of loss in the question he asked the 12, 'Are you going to leave me as well?' (John 6:67). Then, in the final days he was betrayed by one of his close confidants. He was disowned by the man who had been one of his most loyal friends. And all those who should have stood by his side, simply scattered.

And finally, three times, the Bible records that Jesus shows his solidarity with us by being a man of tears. He grieved the loss of one of his closest friends, Lazarus. There is perhaps no more poignant verse that demonstrates Jesus' solidarity with us than when John simply records, 'Jesus wept' (John 11:35). Jesus wept tears of grief for the loss of a man he loved, identifying with all of humanity when death makes us cry. As well as grieving over the loss of an individual, Jesus also wept over the city of Jerusalem (Luke 19:41–44). This grief was due to the lostness of God's chosen people. He was deeply sorrowful that the Jewish nation had, throughout history, consistently rejected God. Finally, in the garden of Gethsemane, Jesus' sweat dropped like tears of blood as he contemplated what he was about to endure on the cross (Luke 22:43–44). He cried out to God for a pathway other than the cross. Yet, in spite of this intense anxiety, Jesus surrendered his will to the will of the Father.

What does this summary demonstrate? Jesus can comfort us in our pain because he endured the full spectrum of human pain. Our God and King doesn't just encourage us along the way as we walk along the valley of the shadow of death. No, he leads us along a pathway that he himself has trod. As Hebrews 4:15 reminds us, we have a High Priest who sympathises with our weaknesses because he himself was tested in every way. When we experience deep pain, we can, in some small way, identify with the pain that he experienced on our behalf.

FREEDOM

A remarkable picture is emerging here. Don't get me wrong, I am not saying that we should seek out painful experiences in order to better understand the suffering of Christ. I don't believe the flagellations of previous generations of Christians is an example to be followed. Rather, in the unexpected and uninvited griefs of life, we have an opportunity to understand the heart of Christ more deeply. And, in this, a surprising result can occur. The late Latin American evangelist, Luis Palau, states, 'we have freedom from our deepest fears because Jesus went deeper than death itself.'[49]

Without diminishing our pain, if we understand that our suffering can bring us into closer identification and more intimate relationship with Jesus, it can bring us freedom. Why? Because we learn that we don't need to resist the grief we are feeling. The depths of our sadness don't have to be fought. Rather, we have the freedom to grieve deeply and in that very place of grief, to experience more deeply the love of God. This is a wonderful mystery that is apprehended by faith. But it is also the testimony of countless Christians throughout the ages who have found peace, freedom and hope in the midst of their deepest trials.

This explains how Raymond Bukenya can still be a man of faith even when facing seemingly insurmountable challenges and how Elizabeth Elliot can develop a global ministry after enduring grief upon grief.

However, in this place of deep pain, we also have to endure deep challenges. There are some harsh realities to walking through the valley of the shadow of death, not least in the area of our human relationships. The next chapter will consider how we face some of these challenges as Christians in the 21st Century.

REFLECT

Consider these words of Psalm 73 quoted above:

'Whom have I in heaven but you?
And earth has nothing I desire besides you.
My flesh and my heart may fail,
but God is the strength of my heart
and my portion for ever.' (Psalm 73:25–26)

What have you learned about God that perhaps you would not have if you hadn't experienced the pain of grief?

How have you felt solidarity with Jesus in your grief?

CHAPTER SIX

LIFE IN THE VALLEY

Every step was reluctant, and time seemed to slow
its pace, so that between the raising of a foot and the
setting of it down minutes of loathing past.

JRR TOLKIEN[50]

THE HEAVIEST BRAIN FOG

The phone rang at 6am. It was life changing news of the worst kind. Danielle Campsall shares her story in the Grief and Grace video series. Her brother had been murdered. Not only did Danielle and her family have to deal with the tragedy of losing her beloved brother but they were also thrown into the whirlwind of the police investigation. Danielle describes the immediate aftermath of her brother's death as 'surreal'. This is surely only something that happens in the movies or that you hear about on the news. Her world had been ripped apart. She'd shared an incredibly close bond with her brother which had now been suddenly and violently torn asunder. The pain of an experience like this is indescribable. Danielle shares that it was as if a fog descended upon her, the heaviest brain fog that she'd ever experienced. She explains, 'you can be in a room full of other people but it feels like you're in a different zone.' She now had to learn to navigate a future she had not chosen. Everything, including her faith, needed to be realigned to her new reality of life without her brother. Danielle describes how she had to make the conscious choice to take hold of her Creator's hand and walk with him on this painful journey. She journaled: 'I'm going to grab hold of his hand and we're going to walk it together.'

LIVING WITH PAIN

Grief changes us. Living after the loss of a loved one is tough. Grief takes us into uncharted waters. We don't know what to expect or how we'll react to different situations. Living with pain is exhausting. The pain of loss can be a consistent emotional drain that impacts our capacity to perform even the simplest tasks. Things that once came easily to us, are now far more complex. This might be extremely frustrating for the grieving person, compounding the challenge of grieving. But it is a reality we have to face. As human beings we need to recognise our limitations. We've seen that as Christians it is appropriate for us to grieve, we are not immune from the pain. And even though we experience solidarity with God in the midst of our pain, this does not mean we can bypass the physical and emotional impact of living with pain. It could be disastrous if we try to push through grief without recognising that living with pain has an impact on our everyday life. One we need to confront.

I came to refer to my life after the death of Laura as 'facing the future I didn't choose'. And it was a massive adjustment. There was the emotional adjustment of losing my wife of 16 years and being a widower, a word I struggled to come to terms with. Then there was the practical adjustment of now being a single dad and alone having to take the responsibility of caring for our three children. Living under the fog of grief impacts our capacity. Things that were simple to do now take incredible effort. This is why the common advice to 'be kind to yourself' when facing life after death is not just a cliché. It is essential for survival.

Every loss carries these kinds of life-altering adjustments. We would never choose to have to face these immensely painful events. However, as I found, the sun still rises the next morning, our bodies still need feeding, the responsibilities and relationships of life do not suddenly evaporate. Rather, we're flung into the immense challenge of navigating our grief while the world continues to turn. And this can magnify our pain.

Danielle called this a 'brain fog'. I called it my new sixth sense, the constant nagging feeling that something is vastly wrong with the world. The brain fog, the sixth sense – they are describing the same thing. It is grief, and living with grief is painful.

THE PROXIMITY PARADOX

One tough challenge when navigating grief is how to handle our relationships with other people. Be they family members, friends, colleagues and even our social media networks; all our human relationships will be impacted by our grief.

George Matheson was a 19th Century pastor and hymn writer. Blind from his youth and having faced grief, loss, and disappointments of many kinds, he was a man who was familiar with the challenges of suffering. He wrote:

> 'Many of us would tearlessly deal with our grief if only we were allowed to do it in private, yet what is so difficult is that most of us are called to exercise patience, not in a bed, but in the open street for all to see. We are called upon to bury our sorrows not in restful inactivity but in active service; in our workplace, while shopping and doing social events… No other way of bearing sorrow is as difficult as this, for it is truly what is meant by running with patience.'[51]

Matheson is highlighting the challenge of navigating public and private grief. If it was difficult enough for him in the 19th Century, how much more challenging is it for us in the digital age? We don't just handle grief 'in the open street for all to see' but on the information super-highway! Social media has provided another platform which those of us who are grieving need to navigate. As Matheson implies, those of us who have been through deep grief often want to curl up into a ball and hide away. However, psychologists tell us that grieving people require social proximity to help facilitate healing. I call this the 'proximity paradox', which expresses the tension between needing to be with people and wanting to be alone.

As Christians, we are part of a community of believers. But even at our churches, well-meaning people can say insensitive things. Even handling the benign question, 'How are you?' can be tough for someone in deep grief. I initially found going to church really difficult after Laura had died. And yet, I knew I had to still remain connected and not detach myself entirely from people. One way I handled the proximity paradox was to arrive at church just after the service started and leave right as it finished, deliberately limiting my interactions to just a few trusted people.

THE WORLD-WIDE-(ENTANGLED)-WEB

Social media is one opportunity for us to connect with other people as we seek to navigate grief and loss. Yet it is also a medium which can magnify the proximity paradox. Social media can provide some comfort as we reach out to our networks through our time of grief, but it can also paradoxically heighten our sense of isolation. I believe, as Christians, we need to consider carefully how we interact on social media at all times and particularly when going through deep pain.

One challenge is that social media is not just a vehicle for us to share what we're going through, but it also exposes us to the pain of others, which can compound our own grief. As one researcher has written, 'Death is becoming a much more public experience… due in part to the introduction of technology.'[52] The reality is that, pre-social media, we tended to lose touch with people as our social circles changed; now we have an increasingly long list of online 'friends'. It is, therefore, simply the mathematics of probability which means we are going to be exposed to more loss and sadness, alongside the frivolity, triviality, and downright ridiculousness of social media.

The breaking of tragic news via social media seems to now be part of everyday life. I first became aware of how social media would change our interaction with grief in 2011. My good friend, Mark Versey, tragically died aged just 38. He had worked with me in Pretoria for three years and had recently moved to London and taken up a new position within our organisation. I heard the news of his passing via telephone from my dad. Later that afternoon I realised I needed to phone some people with the news. As I was calling some friends and colleagues, I realised that word of Mark's passing was spreading very quickly. So, I logged on to my Facebook account and saw that my feed was filling up with post after post about Mark's death. People were sharing tributes, posting photos, or just expressing their painful disbelief that he had died so suddenly. I initially felt a bit stunned as I witnessed this global expression of grief. But I came to realise that it was an amazing testimony to the impact that Mark's life had had. And it was also an incredible comfort to be able to relate to a global community of people through the shrinking world brought about by social media.

That was 2011 and it was the first time I became aware of how social media can be a powerful medium to help people through their grief. However, an equal and opposite danger has emerged as tragedy can become commonplace resulting in us becoming desensitised to our newsfeeds. In the same browsing session, we can see far-flung friends celebrating an engagement or the birth of a baby, while others are announcing that they have cancer or have lost a job. At any point of any day, our lives can be interrupted with uninvited heart-breaking news as friends and loved ones, or even long-lost acquaintances, experience and share their personal pain.

The reality is that social media is here to stay, and it is a vehicle of communication that people going through grief need to navigate. And there is no playbook on how best to do that. Some people lay their hearts bare for all to read through highly personal and emotive posts. When I lost my wife in 2016, I took a different approach. I determined to try to use the platform sensitively and sparingly. It was certainly a comfort to read other people's tributes to Laura and messages of love that came through various online platforms. Someone kindly saved them all for me and printed them out at a later stage. It was also a great vehicle through which to mobilise prayer and support for our family. However, there were many private and personal things that I didn't feel were appropriate for the world-wide-web to be aware of at that time. So, although I browsed regularly, I posted sparingly.

Erin Hope Thompson, clinical psychologist and founding director of The Loss Foundation confirms, 'Grieving via social media accounts is not recommended as a sole source of processing or grieving, given that it can have many pitfalls of its own.'[53] We must also recognise that our social media accounts are not only accessed by believers but our posts are also laid bare to unbelievers. I believe Paul's counsel to the church in Colossae is critical: 'Be wise in the way you act towards outsiders' (Colossians 4:5).

Therefore, in the midst of a tragic storm, I would advise caution in your engagement with social media. Develop a strategy to handle it. I believe the proximity paradox also applies within the cyber-world and the danger is that it can exacerbate your sense of isolation. Your strategy needs to enable you to share appropriately about what you are going through with your broader social network, while also finding ways to connect more deeply and meaningfully with those people you love and trust.

The critical principle is that you feel empowered to utilise social media in ways that help you and doesn't harm you or others. Additionally, although research is indicating that there are many positive advantages to processing grief online, don't allow social media to become your only platform where you seek to process your grief. My experience on social media after losing my wife was largely positive but it was not all-encompassing. Connect with people directly. Seek professional help and consider joining a support group.

GIFTS ALONG THE WAY

I came to see the community of people around me as a gift that God had given me to help me through my journey of pain. Just as I don't see my relationship with God as a crutch, but as a gift of grace, so I began to see people as gifts along the way. These gifts provided both practical, emotional, and medical support. As an example, for weeks after Laura's death, we had people arrive at our house with meals. The kids joked that it's a good job they like lasagne, as we sometimes had it for several days in a row. But it was a practical way in which people provided support for us.

There were people, in my physical and online community, who journeyed with me through the valley of the shadow of death. I learned a beautiful thing, that although the proximity paradox can be a sensitive and challenging reality to navigate, people became the source of God's gracious gifts that helped me along the way. And this led to some breakthroughs at various stages; glimpses of light breaking through my smog. This brought relief, support and even a smidgen of joy in the midst of pain. God has called us to be in community with other believers. We are vulnerable if we try to face our grief alone. It's not always easy. People might unknowingly say the wrong thing. They may occasionally be insensitive. But it's an important decision that we can take not to pull away completely from those who love us and who share in our pain. I feel the guidance of Hebrews is great advice for all seasons of life:

'Let us hold unswervingly to the hope we profess, for he who promised is faithful. And let us consider how we may spur one another on towards love and good deeds, not giving up meeting together, as some are in the habit of doing, but encouraging one another – and all the more as you see the Day approaching.' (Hebrews 10:23–25)

This doesn't mean that someone going through deep grief shouldn't step back from burdensome responsibility. As we've seen already, the journey of grief is unique for everyone. Some people will need to keep relatively active. Some may want to take a complete break. There's no rulebook that applies to everyone. However, I'm advocating a general principle that, hard as it may be, remain connected to trusted friends and keep engaging with Christian community. This may look different from person to person but it could be a lifeline that enables you to endure through the deepest valley.

THE LONG WINDING VALLEY

These past three chapters have sought to acknowledge the painful realities of life after the death of a loved one. We have seen that lamenting is an appropriate response to the loss of a loved one and a natural process to which Christians are not immune. In fact, grieving deeply is a necessary response to the pain we will experience in this life and it is in the depths of our grief that we can encounter the depths of God's love. In fact, there are many lessons God will teach us in the depths that we would not otherwise experience.

Psalm 23 famously states,

> 'Yea, though I walk through the valley of the shadow
> of death,
> I will fear no evil;
> For You are with me;
> Your rod and Your staff, they comfort me.' (Psalm 23:4,
> NKJV)

The assurance that God is with us in the valley provides great comfort. God also provides other people to share the journey with us and provide practical, emotional and spiritual support. However, we have also seen that navigating the valley of the shadow of death is neither easy nor is it a linear experience. There is not simply a start and finish line. There isn't a point we reach where we can say, 'I've now completed this painful season of my life.' CS Lewis seeks to capture the greater complexity of navigating the valley of the shadow of death:

> 'Grief is like a long valley, a winding valley where any
> bend may reveal a totally new landscape. As I've already
> noted, not every bend does. Sometimes the surprise is
> the opposite one; you are presented with exactly the
> same sort of country you thought you had left behind
> miles ago. That is when you wonder whether the valley

isn't a circular trench. But it isn't. There are partial recurrences, but the sequence doesn't repeat.'[54]

I think CS Lewis is trying to say that the valley of death is difficult to navigate and it's also difficult to describe to others. It is a valley we did not choose to enter and it's a valley of twists and turns that we cannot bypass. However, because God is with us in the valley, we have One who can help us, who holds our hand, and in whom we can have hope.

REFLECT

As we transition to the final part of this book, take some time to reflect on how Danielle Campsall described life navigating the painful dark valley:

'As time goes on you have to navigate your new life and that can be really hard at times because that's not a life you ever wanted… it's time to grab hold of the hand of the One who created you and say "yes" to the life you're now facing in spite of everything within you screaming "no"… I'm going to grab hold of his hand and we're going to walk it together… as you do that more and more, [it] does get slightly easier, but it does take time.'

— In spite of your pain, are you taking hold of the One who created you?
— Are you able to say 'yes' to the life you are now facing in spite of everything within you screaming 'no'?
— Are there people walking this road with you? If not, consider reaching out to a friend or contacting your local church to ask about support groups.

PART THREE

PURPOSE

CHAPTER SEVEN

REDEEMING LOVE

In the darkness of seemingly unredeemable situations we often see new rays of faith shining.
MATT WILSON[55]

A REDEMPTIVE WALK

The ten-kilometre walk seemed to be taking an age. The two friends had heavy hearts and spoke in hushed voices. Grief and confusion overwhelmed them as they tried to make sense of recent events. The travellers ignored the other sojourners along the road, oblivious to anything but their own sense of loss. Their conversation centred upon questions that they could not answer. As with most people gripped by grief, they could not understand *why* events had unfolded in such an unexpected and unexplainable manner. Their perspective was cloudy and their pain was raw.

Almost imperceptibly, a fellow traveller began walking alongside them. Initially reluctant to engage in conversation with a stranger, they soon found themselves disarmed by his sympathetic manner. His simple enquiry as to what they were discussing brought them to a standstill, aghast that this man was not aware of the tragedy that had befallen them and everyone in their community. With incredulity, they gave a concise summary of what had happened.

'Jesus of Nazareth… a prophet, powerful in word and deed before God and all the people, was handed over by our chief priests and rulers to be sentenced to death. He was crucified.' Their eyes still downcast and misted over with tears, they got to the crux of their pain and disappointment, '…we had hoped that he was the one who was going to redeem Israel.'[56]

As they resumed their walk, Cleopas and his unnamed friend went on to explain that it was the third day since these things had taken place and now there were confusing rumours of an empty tomb and visions of angels. They had since departed Jerusalem and were heading to Emmaus and could not make sense of any of this.

As the men continued their journey, the stranger unpacked scripture for them and gave them a fresh perspective on the events that have transpired. The gloom of their grief began to lift and was replaced by awe and wonder. Over a simple supper in Emmaus, their 'eyes were opened' and they suddenly realised that their co-traveller is none other than the resurrected Jesus.

I love this story. Well-known as it is, we can sometimes lose the sense of wonder at what is taking place. But the key point I wish to underline is how the pain that the two men were experiencing meant that they struggled to have a biblical perspective on grief and loss. In essence, this is what we've been seeking to address in this book so far. This story provides a great segue into the final part of this book because when our perspective becomes so clouded by our pain, we might fail to be able to discern God's purposes in and through times of suffering. The premise of the final part of this book is that, as believers in Jesus, our pain is not in vain. We have the assurance that God is always at work in our lives and is working out his perfect purposes, even in our suffering. Philippians 2:13 says, 'For it is God who works in you to will and to act in order to fulfil his good purpose.'

The core issue these two men faced as they trudged along to Emmaus was a loss of hope. Up until this point in their lives, they had held a certain perspective on what hope looked like. They believed that the Messiah was going to bring redemption through physical victory over the enemies of Israel. They had believed that Jesus was the Messiah and, therefore, the events of the past few days had completely floored them. Listen again to what they said: '…we had hoped that he was the one who was going to redeem Israel.' Their disillusionment was compounded because they misunderstood how they were going to be redeemed. The expectations they had meant that they failed to realise that pain and suffering could be God's pathway to redemption. From their point of view, Jesus' death seemed like an absolute disaster.

Thankfully, the resurrected Jesus helped them to return to scripture and gain a different perspective. Luke tells us that Jesus took them through the Torah and the Prophets and 'explained to them what was said in all the Scriptures concerning himself' (Luke 24:27). I think they must have been walking pretty slowly to cover all that ground. But through this remarkable Bible study, they gained a fresh understanding of God's purposes in the events that had just transpired. This not only reframed their grief. It also transformed their understanding of redemption.

This final part of the book considers that when we have a biblical perspective on life after death, then we can discern God's purposes. As we've already seen, this doesn't negate the pain and it doesn't mean all our questions will be answered. However, it can help bring us a different outlook on the future. As with the two men who arrived in Emmaus, this fresh outlook on the future can help restore our hope.

COSTLY REDEMPTION

Albert Wolters wrote that to redeem is to 'buy free,' to 'buy back.'[57] The underlying meaning of redemption is that a price is paid in order to secure freedom or in order to restore something that has been damaged or broken.

The theological error of Cleopas and his companion is that they thought Jesus' death could not be the means of redemption. They had expected Jesus to rule the world from a throne rather than to be slaughtered on a cross. They didn't realise that the redemption of Israel required the sacrifice of the innocent lamb of God. Their hope was in a painless redemption. However, as Jesus showed them, the scriptures clearly teach that there is always a price to be paid to secure redemption. Redeeming love is always costly.

A beautiful Old Testament example of redeeming love is the story of Ruth. Having married into an Israelite family that had emigrated to Moab, Ruth was widowed at a young age. Her mother-in-law, Naomi, also a widow, decided to return to Israel and sought to release Ruth from any obligations towards her. However, in the famous phrase, often repeated in weddings three millennia later, Ruth declared, 'Your people will be my people and your God my God' (Ruth 1:16). In spite of her grief, Ruth made this self-sacrificial decision. There didn't seem to be any great sense of hope that redemption would come. In fact, just the opposite. It appears that Naomi and Ruth returned to Israel with a sense of deep grief and even bitterness at what God had allowed to happen to them (see Ruth 1:20–21).

But then Boaz enters the story and the rest, as they say, is history. Boaz is moved by Ruth's commitment to her mother-in-law. We then discover that he has a family connection and under the guidance of Naomi, Ruth and Boaz follow cultural procedures to ensure they act honourably. Boaz becomes Ruth's 'guardian redeemer.' He literally had to buy back all of Naomi's family's property in order to free Naomi from debt and make him eligible to marry Ruth. This was a costly exercise for Boaz. However, Boaz's commitment to Ruth was not simply transactional. It is a love story of note. There is intrigue, chemistry, flirtation and romance which leads to a fruitful marriage.

The story of Boaz and Ruth is not just a great historical love story. It also points to the greatest love story of all, the story of the gospel. Just like Naomi and Ruth, humanity was lost in bitterness and grief, without hope because of our sinfulness. Yet the redeeming love of God bought us back, restores us, and enables us to live a fruitful life in relationship with God. However, the price that God paid for our redemption was eternally more costly than the price Boaz had to pay. In fact, the Old Testament shows us that the price of our freedom was death itself.

The author of Hebrews summarises that forgiveness from sins was secured through the shedding of blood (Hebrews 9:22). Paul unequivocally links the shedding of Jesus' blood to our redemption: 'In him we have redemption through his blood, the forgiveness of sins, in accordance with the riches of God's grace' (Ephesians 1:7). Through Jesus' sacrifice, he has bought our freedom from sin and restored our relationship with God the Father. This is the hope of the gospel and it is freely given as an act of God's grace. Redeeming love is costly.

My intention here is not to dive too deeply into a theology of redemption in terms of the cosmic scope of what Jesus' accomplished.[58] Rather, it is to recognise that this principle of redemption underpins our lives as children of God. The Bible states that our freedom from sin is secured when we believe in Christ and trust in him for the forgiveness of our sin (Romans 8:1–2; Galatians 5:1). We can then boldly claim that we have been redeemed. However, that is not the end. Paul confidently declares that God works for our good in all circumstances (Romans 8:28). There is no situation that God will not redeem for our good.

I believe that God always has a redemptive purpose for our suffering. This is another noteworthy aspect of the Boaz and Ruth love story. Not only does it point to the grand scope of God's redemptive plan for all humanity but it also reminds us that God cares for vulnerable and grieving individuals. Seemingly insignificant people like Ruth can have their pain redeemed because our loving God desires to buy back our grief and loss. As we've seen, he's not the author of our grief. But, if we truly believe in his sovereignty, there is nothing that can happen to his children that he cannot redeem for good purposes. 'No matter how painful the experience may be, God will use it. In his sovereignty nothing is wasted or useless.'[59]

It's an incredible thought that God wants to 'buy back' your grief and pain. What he *pays* to buy our pain is unique in every circumstance as he knows what is ultimately good for us. Again, this may not be what we expect. But, in hindsight, we will see his perfect fingerprints overseeing the redemptive exchange: our grief for his good gifts. His good gifts are many and varied but ultimately God is working in us to form the character of Christ (2 Corinthians 3:18).[60]

PAUSE AND REFLECT

Once again we find ourselves walking on holy ground as we consider these incredible truths of the gospel.

It is worth reflecting on these quotes of Elizabeth Elliot who herself had to learn that God wanted to buy back her grief after the loss of her husband.

'It's through the deepest suffering that God has taught me the deepest lessons.'[61]

'He has a loving purpose. And He can transform something terrible into something wonderful. Suffering is never for nothing.'[62]

'There is, in fact, no redemptive work done anywhere without suffering. And God calls us to stand alongside Him, to offer our sufferings to Him for His transfiguration and to fill up in our poor human flesh.'[63]

Before reading on, there's a difficult question to answer:

Are you willing to accept that God wants to redeem your grief?

If you don't find peace in an affirmative answer to this question, then this final part of this book will be very difficult for you to read. That's not to say you shouldn't read on. Our journey through grief is never linear. It's full of ups and downs, and lots of bends in the road. If you are struggling with the thought that God wants to redeem your grief then reading on is precisely what you should do. If this sparks anger, frustration, confusion, desperation, then that's ok. Finding life after death can feel like a fight for survival. My request is that you stick with it and take heed of these words of wisdom from Pete Greig:

> 'It's a common human tendency to settle in our grief, to redefine the geography of our lives according to the contours of our pain. And of course, when we are bereaved, it's important to stop for a while and lament our loss. It's not healthy to continue as if nothing is wrong. But neither is it helpful to make our disappointment our permanent domain.'[64]

BEAUTY FROM ASHES

The truth of redemption is both brutal and beautiful. Death is brutal. Whether that's physical death or the death of a dream, a job, or a marriage. There is a cross to be borne. And just as the pathway that Jesus took to secure our redemption required him to suffer the most brutal death imaginable, so our pathway to discover God's multi-faceted grace can take us through brutal times of despair.

But finding life after death requires that we accept that God has a redemptive plan that is ultimately beautiful. His love compels him to redeem our pain. He wants to bring something beautiful out of the ashes of our despair. This is the hope that we have as believers in Jesus Christ. The cross is not the end of the story. In fact, it is often only the beginning. The beauty of God's redemptive plan can lead us into experiences of God's grace and mercy that we would never otherwise have had. That's why the valley of the shadow of death was not the end of David's story. Rather, God led him to a place where he could assert, 'Surely goodness and love will follow me all the days of my life, and I will dwell in the house of the Lord for ever' (Psalm 23:6).

One of our favourite passages of scripture at The Message Trust[65] is Isaiah 61:1–3. This has been a motivating passage since we started the South African hub of The Message Trust in 2014. At heart, it is a redemptive promise. In verses 1 and 2 there is a great redemptive proclamation that God will bind up the broken-hearted, bring freedom to captives, release prisoners from darkness and comfort all who mourn. Then in verse 3 there is a specific word for all those who 'grieve in Zion' (in the New Testament context, all those who trust in God), that he will:

'bestow on them a crown of beauty
   instead of ashes,
the oil of joy

   instead of mourning,
 and a garment of praise
   instead of a spirit of despair.' (Isaiah 61:3)

Can you see here the great redemptive exchange that God is promising us? He is going to buy back the ashes of our grief, our mourning and our despair. And in exchange he is granting us beauty, joy and a garment of praise.[66]

He has a divine plan for our life after death. The Bible doesn't have a prescription of what this will look like. It is uniquely personal as part of God's work in each of us individually. But just as we needed to grasp our salvation by faith in Jesus Christ, so we need to have faith that God has not abandoned us to our grief. He will redeem it. Our task is to discern what God is doing to redeem our pain for his purposes.

MY REDEMPTIVE JOURNEY

In the first months after Laura's death, I was simply in survival mode. However, the first glimpses I had that God would redeem my pain was when I started sharing with family and friends about my grief journey. I've never naturally been an 'open book'. Perhaps it's my ingrained British reserve and stiff upper lip. But I have always found it difficult to articulate what I was feeling in different situations. Yet, as I was processing my grief and journaling vociferously, I found that God was giving me a language to help me express my pain. And as I shared what I was going through with other people, it seemed to resonate with them. Two things would then happen simultaneously. I found that what I was sharing seemed to help other people process and express their own griefs and losses, and in that process, I found it was contributing towards my own healing. This didn't happen overnight. In fact, it's with hindsight that I've been able to recognise what was happening. But, undoubtedly, these were the first signs of God redeeming my pain in a very simple way. These indicators of God's redemption enabled me to face the future I didn't choose. As CS Lewis says, sorrow is not a state but a process.[67] God redeems us through the process; it is not a one-time event.

Over time I began to share my story publicly. Then in writing *Grief and Grace* and *Facing the Future We Didn't Choose*,[68] I was able to share more deeply about what God had done in and through my grief process. God's redemptive work in my life continued as he used my gifts of writing and teaching to provide comfort and help to others. This in turn broadened opportunities to connect with people who were going through similar challenges. It was a great encouragement to hear accounts of how my story was a catalyst for other people to allow God to bring healing to their own pain. I learned that redemption is never simply a personal experience. Rather, God's redeeming plan in our own lives will have a ripple effect of influence that will enable others to experience God's grace and redemptive plan in their own situation. This, in turn, brings much glory back to God.

REDEMPTIVE COMMUNITY

In summary, I learned two very important lessons. Firstly, God may often work through our personality and gifts in order to redeem our pain. I suppose this isn't so surprising. As our creator, he knows us best and will have a personalised redemption blueprint for all of us. And secondly, God often seems to bring redemption through our interaction with community. A redemptive quality of our personal suffering is that it can enable us to better understand and support other people in their own pain. We can become the agents of God's redeeming love to a grieving world. It is a very humbling thought that our personal experience of God's redeeming love can influence others towards finding grace and hope in Christ.

A massive danger of grief is that we isolate ourselves from other people and try to struggle through on our own. Rather than becoming isolated in our grief, there is the potential to discover powerful communal cohesion. In U2 frontman Bono's autobiography he expresses their experience after the loss of fellow bandmate, Larry Mullen's, mother: 'we discovered community is found not just in location and culture but in shared experience.'[69]

I would suggest that there is no shared experience as pervasive as grief. We live in a hurting world. It is *the* common human experience that crosses all cultural, generational, gender and any other barriers you can think of. In his love, God redeems our pain in order that we can share that love with others who are hurting. This is one purpose of the church. The church is a gathering of people who have been set free from sin and yet still live with the consequences of living in a sinful and broken world. Although redemption from our sins is a one-time event, we continue to experience the redeeming love of God in our daily lives. He is constantly bringing beauty from ashes. This is a critical part of our testimony to the world. The church is a redeemed community who are witnesses and demonstrators of God's ongoing redeeming love. NT Wright says:

'One might say that this is the vocation of the Church;
to take the sadness of the world and give back no anger;
the sorrow of the world, and give back no bitterness;
the pain of the world, and not sink into self-pity; but to
return forgiveness and love, blessing and joy.'[70]

And we can only be part of this kind of church when we ourselves become open to God's redeeming love. Going through deep grief has left an indelible mark on me. But as a believer in Jesus Christ, I must have hope in his redemptive plan for my life. I am not exempt from his promise to bring beauty from ashes, to help me to find life after death. And neither are you!

REFLECT

Before moving on to the next chapter, why not ask God to enable you to begin to see new rays of faith shining in your life enabling you to believe that God's love can redeem your pain.

Consider praying this redemptive prayer:

'Bright King of Friday and Father Almighty,
Make a roof for me by night and guard me by day.
If you are to bring me along the path
I have never been before,
Make it a pathway for me to the life of glory.'[71]

CHAPTER EIGHT

STARTING OVER

Joy is hidden in sorrow and sorrow in joy. If we try to avoid sorrow at all costs, we may never taste joy.
HENRI NOUWEN[72]

A WALK ON THE BEACH

Muizenberg holds a special place in my heart. On a perfect Cape Town day, when the south-east wind is not pumping, Muizenberg comes alive as Capetonians flock to the beach to enjoy the extensive beach, warm waters and rolling waves. Hundreds of surfers, from beginners to seasoned veterans, take advantage of the favourable waves. The sounds of laughter, the taste of ice cream and the sheer beauty provides an environment that encapsulates joy. It was at Muizenberg that I found solace in the months after Laura's death.

Initially, I would take the kids and spend time with them in the water. I've written in *Grief and Grace* how, at Muizenberg, I learned that joy and pain are two sides of the same coin. My emotions would oscillate between enjoying the children one moment while having pangs of sorrow the next, as I experienced the void in our lives with Laura not being with us. The reality of being a single dad was at times overwhelming. However, Muizenberg was a place where we all began to find a measure of healing.

On occasion, I began to go to Muizenberg on my own. I decided, rather than just helping the children with their surfing, that I would also learn to surf. It was a healthy distraction and something that I thought would have made Laura proud of me. On windy days, when the waves were not conducive to surfing, I would go for long walks along the beach. It was on one such walk that I had a conversation with God that turned out to be a life-changing moment.

This was about six months after Laura had died. Every journey through grief is unique. Mine had been intensely deep. The six months had felt like six years. Quite surprisingly, even soon after Laura had died, some friends asked me if I would consider remarriage. My standard response was that my marriage with Laura had been so rich, that I couldn't contemplate finding that level of fulfilment again. I knew that I wasn't ready to even think about it, so this straight-bat answer helped me get off the hook before I would change the topic.

As I was walking along Muizenberg beach that morning, I felt God affirm me deep in my spirit. I was reflecting on my grief and sensing that I was moving into a different season. I had returned to work. The children were all in their new schools (they had previously been home-schooled). The tears weren't as frequent. I generally didn't feel as sad. I missed Laura deeply but perhaps I could find a way to face this future that I hadn't chosen. It was in that moment that I felt God say to me, 'Tim, my son, you have grieved well.' Don't get me wrong, it wasn't like I felt God was saying I'd passed some kind of test. Rather, it was a gracious affirmation that he was there with me in my grief. From the day Laura died, I had told God that there was no way I could get through this grief on my own. God was reminding me that he'd been my ally every step of the way.

Then I felt him ask me a question. 'What do you want me to do for you, Tim?'

As much as the question was surprising, my response astonished me. From somewhere deep within me I simply said, 'I don't want to be alone.'

Now, maybe if I were a more spiritually-mature person, God would have replied, 'but you're not alone, I am with you.' But God and I both knew what I meant. I went on to say, 'raising my children, being a leader in ministry, and just doing life, is tough on my own.' From that moment on, my heart was open to being married again and I sensed that God was leading me in that direction. I had an assurance that God would guide me on this journey. Even though I still had lots of questions. Even though the thought of meeting and marrying someone else was quite frightening, God gave me an assurance that he was ultimately in charge and that his purposes for my life would be fulfilled. From that moment, I was open to a new future that I hadn't imagined over the previous six months. It was time to start over and trust that God's redeeming love was leading me into new adventures which would contain fresh opportunities as well as fresh challenges.

Now, this chapter is not about remarriage *per se*. This isn't about finding a 'happily ever after' story that makes us feel all warm and fuzzy. This chapter is to give you hope that God does still have a purpose for your life beyond the death of a loved one. It might look completely different from what you imagined. Yet, if we believe everything that has been written in this book so far, then we need to believe that deep grief is not the end of your story. God's redemptive purposes can lead you into new adventures in your life. There are chapters still to be written and he will help you to graciously turn the page to discover it.

FINDING JOY AFTER DEATH

I interviewed Andrew and Alison Cyprianos as part of the Grief and Grace video series. In the early 2000s, Laura and I were members of the same church as them. Andrew was an elder and they were both very active in the church. At that stage I did not know them well, but I clearly remember when the news was shared that their 22-year-old son, Adam, had died in a car accident. When a young person loses their life in such a tragic way it causes ripple effects of shock that impacts whole communities. Andrew, Alison and their remaining son, entered into an unimaginable nightmare as they had to bury their beloved son. In Alison's words, 'That which I feared most had come upon me.'

I only got to know them better in the months following Adam's death. Andrew allowed the ministry I was leading at the time to utilise office space at the premises where he ran his very successful business. He had renamed the building 'Adam House' and asked that, in lieu of rental, we make a monthly contribution to the memorial fund they had established. I remember being struck by their continued faithfulness to God despite the horror of their loss. Twenty years later, Andrew shared in the interview that they had to make a choice.

They were either going to be destroyed by the tragedy, or they had to trust God to give them the strength to overcome it. They believed that, in Christ, nothing is wasted. In other words, they leant into the redeeming love of God to enable them to survive and cling on to life after death.

Alison shared the following experience:

'A couple of days after Adam died I went out into the garden, it was… brilliant blue skies, bright sunshine and I stood outside my bedroom window and looked up and I thought, "God this can't be, the world cannot just be the same as it's always been – do you not understand that my world is finished? People need to know that Alison's son has died"… and I heard God clearly say to me, "But this is where the rubber hits the road – this is where knowing me has to make a difference in your life."'

Clearly, this didn't lessen the emotional trauma she was facing. Yet it gave her a perspective that enabled her to face her pain without losing her faith in God. She went on to recall another poignant moment that she experienced in the weeks after Adam's death: 'I remember the first time I laughed after Adam passed away. I was absolutely appalled [and thought to myself] How can you laugh? You're not a happy person. You've lost your son!'

One of the biggest challenges as life continues after a traumatic event is coping with the resumption of *normal* life. As I mentioned above, in the aftermath of Laura's death, I experienced joy and pain as two sides of the same coin. Whenever I felt the fog of grief lift and found joy in a particular moment, in that same instant my grief could be magnified because I was having to learn to have fun without Laura being present. I discovered that living in this double-sided tension is not necessarily a bad thing. It caused me to lean into God's grace to find the strength for daily life in my new reality.

However, Alison's experience highlights a parallel double-sided reality that can be more problematic. As we move into finding life after death we can experience that happiness and laughter can evoke the flip side of guilt. We can feel that feeling happy is some kind of betrayal of the person we have lost and this can cripple us from entering into the new things that God has for us. Guilt, compounded by regret, can be a barrier to us finding God's purposes for our future.

Andrew and Alison recognised this. They advise, 'In amongst the sadness and tragedy you can experience a joy that

God has for you, he hasn't put you in this situation to cause you to live in desperate sadness… weeping lasts for a night, but joy comes in the morning.'

Often when preachers talk about joy they remind us that the Bible isn't purely talking about having happy feelings. Rather, biblical joy is a deep-rooted trust in God which enables us to experience his peace even in the most tumultuous storm. Paul expresses that he is able to have joy in God in every situation because he has learned the secret of contentment (Philippians 4:10–12). I believe this is all true. However, if you have a deep-set joy, this will, in time, overflow into your overall sense of well-being. In other words, Christians who are grieving should not expect sadness to be their permanent state. Happiness will return. Laughter will come. After all, as we have seen, loved ones who have died in Christ are experiencing the full reality of eternal joy. They would not want us to be denied joy and happiness while we remain on earth. Knowing this is critical if we are to avoid feeling trapped by guilt when we discover happiness again. As we experience the redeeming love of God, we then discover that God is himself restoring and healing us.

LOVING THE OLD, LOVING THE NEW

The Message Trust was founded by Andy Hawthorne and incorporated as a charity in 1992. However, four years prior to that, Andy and his brother Simon, had responded to God's call to initiate a youth outreach in Manchester which they called

'Message '88'. This initiated the movement which continues to grow around the world impacting hard-to reach young people and communities with the gospel. Back in 1988, in a moment of doubt as to whether God could really use Andy in a significant way, God spoke to Andy through Isaiah 43:19–21. These verses have been the bedrock of The Message ever since. In Isaiah 43:19, God says:

> 'See I am doing a new thing! Now it springs up; do you not perceive it? I am making a way in the wilderness and streams in the wasteland…'

God's core mission is to bring restoration. He brings new things out of old, hope out of despair, light out of darkness and death out of life. The Message has been reaching vulnerable young people and communities for over 30 years and we've seen countless stories of God's restoration power in action. God has a cosmic master plan of restoration. *He is making all things new* (Revelation 21:5). And we are included in that plan which, as we have seen in chapter 3, we don't have to wait for the next life to experience.

God wants to do a new thing in our life. The challenge is that we need to perceive it. We need to ask God to give us eyes to see what he is doing, ears to hear what he is saying, a mind to understand and a heart to obey. Then we will be able to discern his perfect purpose for us as he brings fresh streams of living water into our wasteland.

Dallas Willard puts it this way, 'One of the amazing things about the human being is that it is capable of restoration, and indeed of a restoration that makes it somehow more magnificent because it has been ruined.'[73]

I believe that this is the pathway towards acceptance. It's not a word I like to use often because acceptance can imply resignation: 'I can't change it so I'd better just accept it.' I'm not convinced that's a pathway to healing. Rather, if we trust in God's restoration, then we are starting over from a whole different perspective. Acceptance is not resignation. Rather, accepting God's work in our lives, believing that he is in control and trusting him to make all things new, is part of committing ourselves completely into his hands.

From this perspective, it is transformational. It can change how we perceive God's work in our lives in the past, as well as give us a sense of anticipation for what he is going to do in the future. A lightbulb moment for me came when recording the Grief and Grace video series. I shared in chapter 6 about Danielle Campsall's story whose brother was murdered. In the interview she speaks about the process of healing. She describes her own restoration process as follows:

'It's okay to love the new normal. It's okay to love life without the person. It doesn't take away the pain… it's okay to enjoy the new, it doesn't take away from the old. The old's precious and the new is precious too, and that's what God's grace is all about.'

I absolutely love how she expresses this. She shows us that, in God's purposes, there is continuity between the old and the new. And that continuity is love. When we discover that we can love the old without diminishing the new, and we can love the new without having to feel guilty that it in some way counteracts the old, then we have embraced God's restoration. This is because we're acknowledging that God is sovereign over everything that happens to us and this enables us to live with a sense of gratitude for the past and anticipation for the future. As the author of Ecclesiastes discovered, 'He has made everything beautiful in its time' (Ecclesiastes 3:11).

IT DOES TAKE TIME

God's restoration does make things beautiful again. But it does take time and it is impossible to prescribe what the right length of time is. My initial experience of grief was that it felt like life had gone into slow motion. A minute felt like an hour, an hour like a day, and a day like a week. Then, as time went on, I felt a tension. As God was moving me towards a new future, I felt the tension that it was taking me further away from my life with Laura. Again, time felt like an enemy. However, as with everyone I interviewed in the video series, time does eventually bring us into new places and a greater measure of healing, particularly as we walk this journey with the Lord. There is a restorative destination that God wants to lead us to and we can trust him to make things happen at the right time because he himself can redeem time for his purposes.

A few weeks after my walk on the beach described above, I literally had to make room in my heart to love the new. However, it wasn't such a conscious choice; falling in love rarely is! It happened imperceptibly at first. Then, when I realised it was happening, I was somewhat panicky, particularly when I realised I was feeling and acting like a love-stricken teenager. Initially, Christina crept into my life and into my heart. But then there was an explosion of emotion when I realised what was happening and when my kids started asking why I was spending so much time with Christina. Laughter returned to our household as she increasingly hung out with us. She accepted us as a package deal. Christina not only embraced me and the kids but she also honoured Laura's memory. She helped normalise talking as a family about Laura.

Clearly, the journey towards remarriage had its ups and downs (it was mostly ups to be honest!). However, I was so grateful that God had graciously prepared me in the way he did. It was part of his blueprint for my redemption and restoration. And my blueprint is not a model to be followed by others, rather a testimony to God's glorious goodness which can provide you with courage and hope for the unique journey he has for you.

Our route towards remarriage is a topic to be explored more fully elsewhere (invite us out for coffee, we love to share our story). God enabled me to reach a place of gratitude for the life I'd lived with Laura and contentment in the new adventure he had for me. We all miss Laura dearly and I still can't explain why she died so young. Yet I have learned to trust in God's perfect plan. A plan for me, my family and all who loved her.

The pace of restoration is unique for everyone. As with other aspects of the grieving process we've discussed, starting over is not a linear journey. There are twists and turns. However, I can truly say that God has granted me the ability to be able to love my new life to an even greater degree precisely because, having been through deep grief, I've now got a greater appreciation for God's gifts and how precious they are. Starting over is not a callous cutting off of the past. Rather, it's a place of gratitude where we can genuinely thank God for the beautiful chapters he's led us through until this point, while being able to turn the page and embrace the new chapter without guilt or shame. We love the old. We love the new.

On our wedding day, Christina, my beautiful bride, walked down to Brian Johnson's adaption of Psalm 62, 'We Will not be Shaken'. We realised then that the purpose of our new life together would be built upon this timeless promise of God.

'Truly my soul finds rest in God;
my salvation comes from him.
Truly he is my rock and my salvation;
he is my fortress, I will never be shaken.' (Psalm 62:1–2)

God graciously restores those who look to him. And he provides the foundation for us to start over, recognising that in him alone can we find rest for our souls, salvation from fear, and have an unshakeable faith for our future.

REFLECT

Wherever you find yourself in your journey of restoration, take some time to meditate upon this beautiful poem and allow the Holy Spirit to minister to your soul.

Above all, trust in the slow work of God.
We are quite naturally impatient in everything
to reach the end without delay.
We should like to skip the intermediate stages.
We are impatient of being on the way to something
unknown, something new.
And yet it is the law of all progress
that it is made by passing through
some stages of instability –
and that it may take a very long time.
And so I think it is with you;
your ideas mature gradually – let them grow,
let them shape themselves, without undue haste.
Don't try to force them on,
as though you could be today what time
(that is to say, grace and circumstances
acting on your own good will)
will make of you tomorrow.

continues over

Only God could say what this new spirit
gradually forming within you will be.
Give Our Lord the benefit of believing
that his hand is leading you,
and accept the anxiety of feeling yourself
in suspense and incomplete.

— Pierre Teilhard de Chardin

CHAPTER NINE

I AM THE RESURRECTION

You can blow out a candle
But you can't blow out a fire
Once the flames begin to catch
The wind will blow it higher.
PETER GABRIEL[74]

MARTHA'S MOMENT

A mixture of emotions coursed through her veins as she went to meet Jesus. *Disappointment.* Why had he delayed in coming? If he hadn't delayed, maybe everything would be different now. Her brother had now been dead for four days. If Jesus had come sooner, then everything would have been different. *Confusion.* Lazarus was one of his special friends. Surely the Messiah could have healed him. After all, he had healed countless other people who he didn't know like he knew Lazarus. *Sadness.* The grief was overwhelming and raw. She wasn't sure how she could even look Jesus in the eye as hers were still red with tears and her brokenness made her feel vulnerable. Yet, she also experienced a measure of *peace*. Perhaps even *anticipation*. At last, Jesus was here. It was always comforting to be in his presence. All she knew is that when she heard that Jesus had arrived she had to immediately leave what she was doing to go out to meet him. In that moment, she gripped hold of whatever modicum of faith she could muster. She needed to be honest with Jesus. But she hadn't entirely lost hope that, even now, Jesus could bring some light into her darkness.[75]

The ensuing exchange between Martha and Jesus is quite remarkable. Within the context of a conversation with a grieving sister, John records two sentences that provide a foundation of hope for every grieving believer. Jesus says to Martha, 'I am the resurrection and the life. The one who believes in me will live, even though they die; and whoever lives by believing in me will never die' (John 11:25–26). Although Martha didn't immediately understand the full impact of what Jesus was saying, Jesus was gently adjusting her perspective on death. As we saw in chapter 5, Jesus then shared the pain of Martha and her sister, Mary. John recounts that Jesus was 'deeply moved in spirit and troubled' to the extent that he wept with them (John 11:33–35). However, Jesus also knew that his heavenly Father had a purpose to be fulfilled. Jesus had alluded to this before embarking on the trip to Bethany, alerting his disciples to the fact that Lazarus was 'asleep' (see chapter 3), and that he would wake him (John 11:11) in order that they would *believe* (John 11:15). Now in Bethany, Jesus makes the purpose of this seeming tragedy even clearer as he tells Martha, 'Did I not tell you that if you believe, you will see the glory of God?' (John 11:40).

We are familiar with what happens next. Jesus demonstrates the truth of this statement by calling Lazarus to come out of his tomb. Having been dead for four days, the Messiah called his friend back to life. Through this miracle, Jesus gave a foretaste of the resurrection power that is available to all who believe in him.

Simultaneously, the raising of Lazarus accelerated the work of Jesus' enemies and shortly after Lazarus' resurrection, Jesus himself was in a tomb. If that tomb had remained closed, then in spite of the miracle Jesus had performed in raising Lazarus, his words to Martha would have ultimately been powerless. However, on the third day, the tomb was opened and Jesus was powerfully and eternally resurrected. Unlike Lazarus and all those Christ raised during his earthly ministry, Jesus didn't have to face physical death again. Rather, he triumphantly ascended to heaven (Acts 1:9).

As Peter would declare, just a few weeks later,

'God raised this Jesus to life, and we are all witnesses of it. Exalted to the right hand of God, he has received from the Father the promised Holy Spirit and has poured out what you now see and hear.' (Acts 2:32)

Thus, a new era of history began. The post-resurrection era in which we have the privilege of living and dying. Frank Viola says, 'his resurrection tells us that he is the beginning of the new creation; his ascension tells us that he is now in charge.'[76] Now all those who believe in Christ get to experience a dual reality. When we die, we will live. And while we are living, we have the assurance that we will never die.

The Christian faith is built upon the assurance that Jesus Christ has conquered death. The great enemy was defeated by Jesus. He carried our sin on the cross. And he was victorious over death through the resurrection. Once for all. He then ascended to reign with his Father in heaven. Jesus was God's answer to the Psalmist's cry:

> 'The cords of death entangled me, the anguish of the grave came over me; I was overcome by distress and sorrow. Then I called on the name of the LORD: 'Lord, save me!' (Psalm 116:3–4)

Through Jesus, we have been saved from the entangling cords of death.

RESURRECTION: PERSPECTIVE, PAIN AND PURPOSE

Jesus told Martha, 'I am the resurrection and the life.' And these are his words to all of us who have experienced deep loss. Whatever form of grief you are experiencing, it could be helpful to imagine yourself in Martha's shoes. You rise from your disillusionment, confusion and pain to approach Jesus. In your darkest moment you blurt out to him, 'If only you had been here.' Perhaps you can glimpse the compassion in his eyes as he reminds you, 'Your loved one will rise again.' As you seek to clutch on to those words in faith he then assures you, 'I am the resurrection and the life. The one who believes in me will live, even though they die.'

Encountering Jesus in this way is transformational. Through the lens of understanding Jesus as the resurrection and the life, we are able to truly find life after death. This is ultimately how we navigate a biblical path as we've sought to do through the three parts of this book. In the light of the resurrection, we can adjust our perspective, process our pain, and discover God's purposes. Or perhaps, more accurately, as Martha herself discovered, in the *presence* of the resurrected Christ we can adjust our perspective, process our pain, and discover God's purposes. And just as Jesus said to Martha, so he gently says to us, 'Did I not tell you that if you believe, you will see the glory of God?'

This is a remarkable thought isn't it? God's purpose for us is to see the glory of God at work even in and through life's most painful experiences. But this is only possible if we *believe*. We must believe that the resurrected Christ is alive, able and willing to infuse his resurrection power into our brokenness. The result is not only that we can have our pain redeemed and our hearts restored. But, in so doing, the resurrected Jesus brings glory to God.

ANSWERING THE WHY

Many times in this book I've acknowledged the challenge that we can't answer the 'why' questions. Why do those we love, suffer and die? Why do we endure so much grief in this life? Why does it seem that our prayers are not always answered in the way we would like? Why is there injustice that indiscriminately impacts believers alongside unbelievers? Why did God allow something to happen that he had the power to stop?

Perhaps you will never know the specific 'why' relating to the circumstances you are facing. But, as a believer in the resurrected Jesus Christ, there is a purpose we can discover in our suffering that helps us answer why God allows us to face grief and loss.

Why does God allow his children to suffer? Because he wants us to know and experience the power of the resurrection in our circumstances. He wants us to understand that believing in Jesus is not wishy-washy. Rather, our faith in the resurrected Jesus not only helps us to survive *through* grief but find victory over grief in a way that will bring glory to God.

When I interviewed people who had suffered tremendous loss as part of the Grief and Grace video series, I was struck that each testimony was a story of victory in spite of tragedy. Each of the people who had endured unbelievable pain had come to a place where they were able to celebrate God's goodness in their lives in spite of the grief they had experienced. In fact, it appeared to me that each of them had become stronger in their faith and more effective in their service of Christ precisely because God had allowed them to walk through the valley of the shadow of death. Not one of them would have chosen to face what they had to endure. However, all of them recognised that God had used the situation to shape them into the people they had become. This enabled them to become grateful. And in their gratitude, God is glorified.

A RESURRECTION PERSPECTIVE

Did you notice in Jesus' words to Martha that the resurrection has a double-edged perspective for those who believe? Jesus' promise assures us that those who have died in Christ are now living in him. And it assures those of us who are still to face physical death, that we will never die.

There is a dual reality here that comes into clear focus. Because of the resurrection of Jesus:

We have hope that those who have died are now with him and experiencing eternal joy. For them, **it's just the beginning of their story**.

and

Those of us who remain on earth can find life beyond our grief and discover purpose in spite of our pain. For us, **it's not the end of the story**.

I will conclude this book by considering both of these assertions, starting with the second statement first.

IT'S NOT THE END OF THE STORY

There's a delightful film called *The Best Exotic Marigold Hotel*. It depicts seven elderly British tourists who respond to an advert inviting them to retire in Jaipur, India. Unfortunately, the hotel does not live up to expectations and they find themselves in a rundown, decrepit hotel. It is here where their lives intertwine with one another, and their delightful host called Sonny. Sonny has a sunny disposition and is an eternal optimist who has a memorable catchphrase. Whenever a situation seems hopeless or a person is despondent, he quips, 'Everything will be all right in the end... if it's not all right then it's not the end.'

I like the simplistic optimism of this phrase. Clearly, it's not something to quote to someone who is going through deep grief as such an inappropriate and flippant remark could be quite offensive. However, what I want to underline is that, for a believer, death is not the end of our story. We believe in resurrection life and because of our hope in the resurrection, death is merely one moment in a far bigger narrative. I believe the same is true for when we are grieving. We do not need to be defined by loss. Rather, we can let God work in us when we are grieving. We can trust him to be shaping us as he brings healing. Grief is not the end of the story. The same Spirit who raised Jesus from the dead is at work in us and can bring resurrection power into our grief in order that we can find life after death and live for the purpose of bringing glory to God (Romans 6:10–11). As I've made abundantly clear throughout this book, this doesn't belittle our pain. Rather, it enables us to trust that God has a purpose beyond our pain because our pain is not the end of the story.

As our story continues to unfold, grief can have different shades. I've experienced this. In this book I've described some of the deep grief I went through and I've also shared about how God has brought healing that has helped me start over. However, there are still moments when I once again sense the shadow of grief cast over my heart. Whether prompted by a particular memory of Laura, the experience of others, or seeing my own children still navigate their own painful journey, grief continues to be a process. However, it is one that I know God can use in my life to help me understand his grace and mercy to a deeper degree. Frank Viola says, '...for the Christian, suffering has a special purpose. It's the chiselling of God designed to transform you into the image of His Son.'[77] Hudson Taylor, the great 19th Century missionary to China, concurs, 'Trials afford God a platform for his working in our lives. Without them I would never know how kind, how powerful, how gracious he is.'[78] Being chiselled is not fun. But I recognise it is a necessary part of my discipleship as God chips away at my self-sufficiency, pride, ego, and various idolatries, in order to form me more into the likeness of Christ. Although I don't welcome pain, I do welcome his gracious work in my life. It means he's not finished with me yet. My story is still unfolding and, as it does, I trust and pray that it will bring glory to God. In commentating on the biblical narrative of the death of Lazarus, Bruce Milne writes, 'We can offer our trials to God for him either to remove or retain as *he* pleases, thereby bringing glory to his name and deepening our faith, and possibly that of others too.'[79]

I trust that this book has encouraged you that your pain and grief is not the end of the story for you but part of a deep work that God wants to do in and through you. I trust that you have found that the Bible provides an eternal perspective that can serve as your survivor's guide in and through the toughest of times. To that end, consider this gem from Lamentations. The majority of this book contains Jeremiah's poetic laments as he traversed his own emotional trauma following the destruction of Jerusalem. However, in chapter 3, he nailed his colours to the mast that he would trust in God's ultimate purposes in spite of his circumstances.

'For no one is cast off
by the Lord forever.
Though he brings grief, he will show compassion,
so great is his unfailing love.
For he does not willingly bring affliction
or grief to anyone.' (Lamentations 3:31–33)

God has a purpose beyond your pain. Hold on in faith that you have not been cast off and that you will experience his compassion and unfailing love to ever-increasing degrees.

IT'S JUST THE BEGINNING
OF THE STORY

And finally, we have hope because, for those who die in Christ, it is only the beginning of the story.

I have read through CS Lewis' *The Chronicles of Narnia* series to each of my older children and will no doubt read through them all once more with my youngest child when she is old enough. The final book of the series is called *The Last Battle*. I am not going to apologise for the spoiler that is to come. Funnily enough, I first read *The Last Battle* as a child when I was in hospital recovering from having my tonsils removed. For some reason, my parents bought me the last book in the series before I'd read any of the others. I dutifully read it but didn't really have a clue what was going on. However, I've now read it several times and, although a children's book, I find that I get fresh insights from Lewis' allegory every time I read it.

Having followed the fortunes of various children moving between our world and the parallel world of Narnia, *The Last Battle* brings the series to a climax as the final war in Narnia ensues which precursors the end of the old world of Narnia. Aslan, the lion whose willing sacrifice had conquered death in the earlier story, *The Lion, The Witch and The Wardrobe*, now provides a doorway from Narnia into his *real* country for those who had faithfully followed him. If you haven't read the book, it provides a beautiful depiction of both the continuity between this life and the next, as well as the transformation that will occur. Lewis then concludes with these words:

'And as He [Aslan] spoke, He no longer looked to them like a lion; but the things that began to happen after that were so great and beautiful that I cannot write them. And for us this is the end of all the stories, and we can most truly say that they all lived happily ever after. But for them it was only the beginning of the real story. All their life in this world and all their adventures in Narnia had only been the cover and the title page: now at last they were beginning Chapter One of the Great Story which no one on earth has read: which goes on for ever: in which every chapter is better than the one before.'[80]

For those who have died in Christ we can truly say that this life was just the cover and the title page. Though lost to us temporarily in this world, in the perspective of eternity it will just be a blink of the eyes until we are reunited with them. This is the destiny of all those who believe in Jesus and that's when our true story begins. Yes, there will be continuity with this life. But there is also complete transformation. The Apostle Paul describes it like this:

'Listen, I tell you a mystery: We will not all sleep, but we will all be changed – in a flash, in the twinkling of an eye, at the last trumpet. For the trumpet will sound, the dead will be raised imperishable, and we will be changed. For the perishable must clothe itself with the imperishable, and the mortal with immortality. When the perishable has been clothed with the imperishable, and the mortal with immortality, then the saying that is written will come true: "Death has been swallowed up in victory."

"Where, O death, is your victory?

Where, O death, is your sting?"

The sting of death is sin, and the power of sin is the law. But thanks be to God! He gives us the victory through our Lord Jesus Christ.' (1 Corinthians 15:51–57)

Resurrection life is promised to all who believe. Our mortality will be clothed with Christ's immortality. This is God's ultimate purpose. We will all receive a resurrection body and live eternally in his presence. We have the assurance that death has been defeated by Christ's work on the cross.

One day, God will turn the page of history and we will experience a whole new reality. It's beyond my capability to describe it. But we can believe and trust that, on that day, we will truly understand that our story has only just begun.

Ultimately, we find life after the death of a loved one by believing in the eternal life that Jesus has promised us. The Bible is our guide on this pathway and will move us beyond survival to thriving as God's children both now and forever.

And as the champion of the eternal story of grace, let's leave the final word to Jesus. My prayer is that we will all find the courage and strength to trust in him who holds the key to us finding life after death!

'I am the living one. I died, but look – I am alive forever
and ever!
And I hold the keys of death and the grave.'
(Revelation 1:18, NLT)

REFLECT

For our final reflection, meditate upon the following
Bible verses. Consider how these passages shape our
perspective, help us process our pain and reveal God's
purpose.

'I consider that our present sufferings are not worth
comparing with the glory that will be revealed in us. For
the creation waits in eager expectation for the children
of God to be revealed. For the creation was subjected
to frustration, not by its own choice, but by the will of
the one who subjected it, in hope that the creation itself
will be liberated from its bondage to decay and brought
into the freedom and glory of the children of God.'
(Romans 8:18–21)

'But because of his great love for us, God who is rich
in mercy, made us alive with Christ even when we were
dead in transgressions – it is by grace you have been
saved. And God raised us up with Christ and seated

us with him in the heavenly realms in Christ Jesus, in order that in the coming ages he might show the incomparable riches of his grace, expressed in his kindness to us in Christ Jesus.' (Ephesians 2:4-7)

Consider writing your own prayer, poem, song, or perhaps your testimony, expressing your heart to God in response to what you have experienced/learned in reading this book.

Feel free to send your feedback to me:

www.griefandgrace.org

ACKNOWLEDGEMENTS

Writing a book is a team effort. I'd like to specifically thank the following people:

David Tucker. Not only do you provide invaluable assistance as an editor and proofreader, but I particularly appreciate your thoughtful interaction with the material and your enthusiastic encouragement.

Mahlatse Mashua. Your foreword is quite remarkable. It took my breath away when I first read it. Thank you so much for taking the time to engage with the content of this book in such a meaningful way. I trust that your example will inspire everyone else who reads *Finding Life After Death*.

I want to particularly thank the following people for allowing me to share some of their own journey of finding life after death stories: Gareth Simpson, Raymond Bukenya, Andrew and Alison Cyprianos and Danielle Campsall.

To the following people for giving feedback before we completed the final draft: Roger Tucker, Gareth Lloyd-Jones, Dalene Reyburn, Andy Hawthorne, Dianne Matthews, John

Patterson, Paul Hallam, Chris Bolinger, Bekele Shanko, Luxolo Kentane.

And to two people who ensured the final product was ready for release: Sylvia Johnson, thanks for enthusiastically volunteering to do the proofreading. Simon Baker from Thirteen Creative for how you convert the manuscript into a beautifully crafted end product.

Finally, a special mention to Shaun Pretorius. You are the definition of a true friend.

NOTES

1   JK Rowling, *Harry Potter and the Half Blood Prince* (Pottermore Publishing: Kindle edition), Location 7130.

2   Samantha Kemp-Jackson, 'The Uncomfortable Reality of Social Media Mourning', https://medium.com/swlh/the-uncomfortable-reality-of-social-media-mourning-3111fe4bf18f.

3   Frank Viola, *God's Favourite Place on Earth* (David C Cook: 2013), 116.

4   Bono, *Surrender* (Knopf: 2022), 48.

5   CS Lewis, *A Grief Observed* (Faber and Faber: 1961), 11.

6   Quoted in Larry Loftis, *Code Name: Lise* (Mirror Books: 2019), 155.

7   Bruce Milne describes God's sovereignty as follows: 'He rules in the world and his will is the final cause of all things, including specifically creation and preservation (Ps. 95:6; Rev. 4:11), human government (Pr. 21:1; Dn. 4:35), the salvation of God's people (Rom. 8:29f.; Eph. 1:4, 11), the sufferings of Christ (Lk. 22:42; Acts 3:23), the sufferings of Christians (Phil. 1:29; 1 Pet. 3:17), man's life and destiny (Acts 18:21; Rom. 15:32) and even the smallest details of life (Mt. 10:29). God reigns in his universe, exalted over all other claimants to power and authority. He alone is God: 'I am the LORD, and there is no other' (Is. 45:6; cf. 43:11; 44:8; 45:21).' Bruce Milne, *Know the Truth* (Inter-Varsity Press: 1982), 66.

8   'God's kingdom is not just his rule and reign. It is his redemptive rule and reign; it's the loving sovereignty he exercises over his own people.' Greg Gilbert, *What is the Gospel?* (Crossway: 2010), 87.

9   I find the Psalms particularly helpful when going through grief. They are such an honest reflection on the struggles of faith within the context of suffering. Dallas Willard wrote, '[the Psalms] do not promise that we will have no trials, as human beings understand trials. They promise, instead, totally unbroken care, along with God-given adequacy to whatever happens.' Dallas Willard, *The Divine Conspiracy* (Harper Collins: 2009), 292.

10   CS Lewis, *A Grief Observed*, 16.

11   It's impossible to read the book of Job and not be struck by God's sovereignty. Nothing takes God by surprise and he works through everything that happens for Job's ultimate good and for his own glory.

12   Krish Kandiah, *Paradoxology* (Hodder & Stoughton: 2014), 95.

13   Kandiah, *Paradoxology*, 96.

14   Quoted in Philip Yancey, *Soul Survivor* (Waterbrook: 2003), 29.

15   Yancey, *Soul Survivor*, 28–29. Emphasis added.

16   David Platt, *Radical* (Multnomah Books: 2011), 180.

17   Dallas Willard, *The Divine Conspiracy*, 296.

18   Brennan Manning, *The Ragamuffin Gospel* (Authentic Media: 2004), 42.

19   For example, the opening verse of 'Swing Low, Sweet Chariot': 'I looked over Jordan, and what did I see / Coming for to carry me home / A band of angels coming after me / Coming for to carry me home.'

20   See Romans 8:11.

21 For example, read Jesus' parables in Matthew 13 and 25 for several examples where Jesus teaches on the kingdom of heaven.

22 A helpful book that explores everything the Bible teaches about heaven is Randy Alcorn's *Heaven: A Comprehensive Guide to Everything the Bible says about our Eternal Home* (Tyndale: 2004).

23 Willard, *The Divine Conspiracy*, 59.

24 Willard, *The Divine Conspiracy*, 98.

25 Randy Alcorn, *Heaven*, 8.

26 Andy Hawthorne, *A Burning Heart* (The Message Trust: 2002), 217.

27 NT Wright, *The Crown and the Fire* (Wm B Eerdmans: 1992), 108.

28 Dane Ortlund, *Gentle and Lowly* (Crossway: 2020), 195.

29 Dallas Willard, *Renovation of the Heart* (Navpress: 2002), 71. I would just add a caution here. I don't believe Mueller is saying not to consider the counsel of other people – particularly believing friends and family members. The Bible often exhorts us to listen to the opinion of others (e.g. Proverbs 15:22). Rather, he is talking about being willing to stand for God and endeavour to live a righteous life in spite of the criticism and even rejection of others. Also see Jesus' words in Luke 14:26–27.

30 Watchman Nee, *The Normal Christian Life* (Hendrickson Publishers: 2006), 23.

31 Alcorn goes on to say: 'Seeing God will be like seeing everything else for the first time. We will discover that seeing God is our greatest joy, and life itself. Every other joy of Heaven will be derivative, flowing from the fountain of our relationship with God.' Randy Alcorn, *Heaven*, 15.

32 For example, see: Matthew 5:29–30, 10:28–33, 25:41–46; Luke 13:22–30; John 3:16–21, 36.

33   Bono, *Surrender*, 135.

34   Teresa of Avila, *The Life of Saint Teresa of Avila* (Penguin Group: 1956), 56.

35   Mark Vroegop, *Dark Clouds, Deep Mercy* (Crossway: 2019), 26.

36   CS Lewis, *A Grief Observed*, 39.

37   Michelle Obama, *Becoming* (Crown Publishing Group: 2018), 144.

38   Henry Cloud, *Necessary Endings* (Harper Business: 2011), 215.

39   Mark Vroegop, *Dark Clouds*, 26.

40   *Deep Calls Unto Deep No. 865, A Sermon Delivered On Lord's-Day Morning, April 11, 1869*, By CH Spurgeon, At The Metropolitan Tabernacle.

41   Details taken from Raymond Bukenya's account in his Master's thesis: 'Towards An African Apologetic – The Missiological Value Of A Decolonized Response To The Existential Dilemma Of Suffering And Pain; A Case Study Of The Karimojong People Of Northeastern Uganda' (2023).

42   Bukenya, 'Towards An African Apologetic', 18.

43   Almost all commentators believe that the psalmists were probably in some way physically cut off from being able to worship in the tabernacle/temple in Jerusalem. They were thus feeling the pain of being devoid of the sense of God's presence.

44   Joni Eareckson Tada says, 'When we are in pain, God feels the sting in his chest,' cited in the foreword to Elizabeth Elliot, *Suffering is Never for Nothing* (B&H Publishing Group: 2019), 12.

45   Elizabeth Elliot, *Suffering is Never for Nothing*, 12.

46   Isaiah 54–66 goes on to reveal the innumerable redemptive benefits that came as a result of the servant's obedience.

47 See Luke 22:35–38 where Jesus states that he would fulfil the words of the prophecy. In Acts 8:26–35, the Ethiopian eunuch becomes a believer as Philip explains how Jesus fulfilled Isaiah 53. Peter references Isaiah 53 when teaching on unjust suffering in 1 Peter 2:19–25.

48 Dane Ortlund, *Gentle and Lowly*, 57.

49 Luis Palau, *A Life on Fire* (Zondervan: 2019), 204.

50 JRR Tolkien, *The Two Towers* (HarperCollins: 2008), 145.

51 George Matheson, *Streams in the Desert* (Zondervan: 2016), 408.

52 Resa Ware, 'The Impact of Social Media on the Grieving Process' (Master's thesis, 2016).

53 Erin Hope Thompson quoted in 'The Psychological Effects of Grieving on Social Media', https://www.vice.com/en/article/pan4gy/the-psychological-effects-of-grieving-on-social-media

54 CS Lewis, *A Grief Observed*, 46.

55 Matt Wilson, *Concrete Faith* (The Message Trust: 2012), 75.

56 See Luke 24:13–24.

57 Albert Wolters, *Creation Regained* ((Wm B Eerdmans: 1985), 69.

58 'Redemption… is the recovery of creational goodness through the annulment of sin and the effort toward the progressive removal of its effects everywhere.' Wolters, *Creation Regained*, 83.

59 Raymond Brown, *The Message of Hebrews* (Inter-Varsity Press: 1982), 234.

60 'Adversity sometimes helps us to enter more fully into our indebtedness to God, our partnership with Christ and our reliance on the Spirit. In this way we can the more fully share his holiness.' Brown, *The Message of Hebrews*, 235

61 Elizabeth Elliot, *Suffering is Never for Nothing*, 12.

62 Elizabeth Elliot, *Suffering is Never for Nothing*, 12.

63 Elizabeth Elliot, *Suffering is Never for Nothing*, 89.

64 Pete Greig, *Dirty Glory* (Hodder & Stoughton: 2016), 124.

65 The Message Trust is the ministry in which I serve and publisher of this book.

66 It is not surprising that Jesus utilised this verse at the onset of his public ministry (see Luke 4:18ff). He was nailing his colours to the mast that he was on earth to fulfil God's redemptive plan.

67 CS Lewis, *A Grief Observed*, 46.

68 My adaptation of *Grief and Grace* specifically written as a response to the Covid-19 pandemic.

69 Bono, *Surrender*, 166.

70 NT Wright, *The Crown and the Fire*, 52.

71 Irish prayer quoted by David Pott, *Thoughts on Dying Well* (unpublished), 7.

72 Henri JM Nouwen, *Bread for the Journey: A Daybook of Wisdom and Faith* (HarperOne: 2006), 2.

73 Dallas Willard, *Renovation of the Heart*, 63.

74 Peter Gabriel, 'Biko' (Charisma Records: 1980).

75 See John 11:1–28.

76 Frank Viola, *God's Favourite Place on Earth* (David C Cook: 2013), 175.

77 Frank Viola, *God's Favourite Place on Earth*, 93.

78 Quoted in Bruce Milne, *The Message of John* (Inter-Varsity Press: 1993), 158.

79 Quoted in Bruce Milne, *The Message of John*, 158.

80 CS Lewis, *The Last Battle* (Scholastic: 1995), 224.

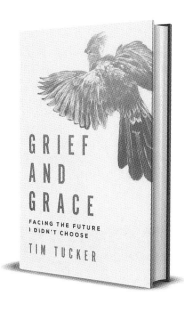

Grief and Grace is the account of a six-month period in Tim Tucker's life when he faced the unimaginable loss: losing his 38-year-old wife to a brain aneurysm. Laura Tucker passed away on the 18 August 2016, leaving behind Tim and their three children. This is a frank and poignant story of how grief and grace can mingle and coexist as Tim faced the future he didn't choose.

Tim has written this book in order to help bring courage and faith to those who face seemingly insurmountable challenges.

Buy the book and explore additional resources:

GRIEFANDGRACE.ORG

Also available from Amazon.com in print and on Kindle.

The Message Trust is a worldwide movement passionately sharing the love of Jesus Christ in words and actions with the hardest-to-reach young people and communities.

Find out more about our global hubs:
MESSAGEGLOBAL.ORG

Contact Tim for speaking engagements:
AFRICA@MESSAGEGLOBAL.ORG